KNITTING
WILD

THERESSA SILVER

Theressa J. Silver Press
Oregon

KNITTING WILD

ISBN-13: 978-1-7335704-0-4

Second Edition
Published by Theressa J. Silver Press

Copy Editor: Stephen B. Gerken
Models: Chelsea Rinaldi, Lacy Schreiber, Reba Sparrow, and Robin Gill
Sample Knitters: Erica Stuart, Kate Lindstrom, Lilie Wells, and Mesha
McMullen
Technical Editor: Andi Smith

Every effort has been made to ensure that all the information in this book
is accurate at the time of publication. However, Theressa J. Silver Press
neither endorses nor guarantees the content of external links referenced
in this book.

If you have questions or comments about this book, or need information
about licensing, custom editions, special sales, or academic/corporate
purchases, please contact Theressa J. Silver Press: tsilver@spiretech.com

This book is dedicated to three mentors
who nurtured my curiosity and encouraged
my interest in the natural world.

Donald Bockler "Doc Boc"
Dr. Frank Gwilliam
Dr. Richard Forbes

TABLE OF CONTENTS

PATTERNS

Howl 16

Cuyahoga Canals 42

Splays 62

Trillium 30

Whoop! Whoop! 50

Here Be Puffins 70

Deciduous 36

Pihemanu 56

Mangrove 76

Sage-Grouse 88

Glacier 114

Conks 136

Milkweed and Monarchs 96

Painted Desert 122

Muskox 144

Synchronous Firefly 106

Fumarole 130

About the Photography

Photography is an integral part of any knitting pattern book. For *Knitting Wild* it was important to me that the photographs not only capture the beauty and design elements of the knit items, but also incorporate a feeling of wildness. Marilyn Barnes is both a nature photographer and a knitter, and was the perfect choice for this project. In keeping with the themes of "wild places" and "conservation land," we chose two urban wildlife refuges in Portland, Oregon as our photo shoot locations.

The first photo shoot took place in the Reed College Canyon. Located in the middle of the Reed College campus and protecting the headwaters of Crystal Spring, this 28-acre refuge has undergone significant restoration efforts in recent years. It is home to a growing number of plant and animal species. The second photo shoot took place in the 142-acre Oaks Bottom Wildlife Refuge located along the Willamette River. The refuge was created in 1969 to protect one of the last areas of marshland within Portland's city limits. Today it is managed by Portland Parks and Recreation and is a lovely spot for hiking and bird watching.

One of my goals for this book is to create a sense of "ownership" in my readers. The natural world belongs to all of us, to enjoy and to protect. I wanted to incorporate images of the natural world as captured by members of our own community. I wanted to show what was important and interesting from other perspectives besides my own. With that in mind, I put out a call for submissions for nature photographs. I was not disappointed. Throughout the book you will find photographs taken by members of our community celebrating the natural places they love. The variety of locations and subject matter represented in these photos illustrates the vastness of the natural world that we are tasked with protecting.

LIST OF CONTRIBUTED PHOTOS

INTRODUCTION: WHY THIS BOOK

Knitting Wild is a book of knitting patterns inspired by and dedicated to the wild beauty of America's national parks and wildlife refuges. It is a lush collection of hats, mitts, shawls, scarves, and cowls that are fun to knit and to wear. There are 21 patterns, each accompanied by information about the place that served as its inspiration. Also included in the book are discussions of how human activities affect the natural world, why this matters, and what we can do about it.

The patterns showcase unique aspects of each location and serve to highlights issues of climate change, habitat conservation, and endangered species protection. I've included a wide range of parks and refuges. Some, like Yellowstone and Great Smoky National Parks, many readers will have visited. Others, like the Midway Atoll National Wildlife Refuge, are so out of the way that most of us will only visit them in photos. It is my hope that this book will inspire knitters to think about these wild places and the threats they face, and to take action to help preserve wildlife, not only in parks and refuges, but also in their own backyards and neighborhoods.

Before I took up knitting, I earned bachelor's and master's degrees in biology. While I did not fulfill my dream of being a research scientist, I have maintained my love of and keen interest in the living world around me. My focus was on animal behavior and how that behavior affects and is affected by the environment within which the animals live. The world is an endlessly fascinating web of minute interconnections and I can't help but draw inspiration from it.

This book has allowed me an opportunity to really let my imagination go wild (puns are always intended), exploring shape and texture in my designs. At the same time, it has given me a place to share my love of and concerns for the natural world with my readers. *Knitting Wild* is a labor of love, combining two things that truly fascinate and inspire me. I hope you will enjoy reading the book and knitting the patterns as much as I have enjoyed creating them.

COLTER'S HELL: THE PLACE THAT STARTED IT ALL

In 1872, President Ulysses S. Grant signed the act of dedication into law, creating Yellowstone National Park. While this was by no means the beginning of the conservation movement in this country, the formation of Yellowstone did signal a growing desire to set aside wild places for the use and enjoyment of all. The initial mission for the park was to preserve it as a "pleasure ground," protecting its unique landscape from being ravaged by entrepreneurs who would strip it for souvenirs.

The Grand Canyon of the Yellowstone

However, the initial legislation only nominally protected the wildlife in the park. The park superintendent lacked both money and resources, and poaching continued in Yellowstone largely unabated. Dr George Bird Grinnell, an early advocate of wildlife conservation, observed that in the winter of 1874–1875, not less than 3,000 buffalo, mule deer, elk, and antelope were taken.

Sapphire Pool

KNITTING WILD

In 1887, Dr Grinnell teamed up with Theodore Roosevelt to form the Boone and Crockett Club. This was an elite club composed of the country's most prominent explorers, writers, scientists, and politicians. They used their considerable influence to encourage the federal government to take steps to protect big game. They championed the Yellowstone Protection Act, which was signed into law by President Cleveland in 1894. This made the park an inviolate wildlife refuge, prohibiting any activities that would harm the wildlife living there. Killing wildlife within the park now carried jail sentences and fines. Finally, two decades after its inception, Yellowstone National Park was truly protected as a wild place, set aside from exploitation, and preserved for all to enjoy for many generations to come.

Bison in Yellowstone

Yellowstone's extreme landscapes and geothermal features defy belief and fuel the imagination. The landscape is so otherworldly that early reports were shrugged off as exaggeration or delusion. In 1809 John Colter, one of the first Europeans to see the area, described it as a place of "fire and brimstone," earning Yellowstone the nickname of "Colter's Hell."

Northern Pacific Railway Brochure; Photo: National Park Service.

In 1885, in an attempt to bring in more customers, The Northern Pacific Railroad published a tourist brochure, "Alice's Adventures in the New Wonderland." This beautifully illustrated brochure featured a letter from the now adult Alice to her friend Edith in which she describes the amazing sights that a visitor would witness on a trip to Yellowstone.

Today, Yellowstone is still a wonderland. Wildlife abounds and with a little patience, visitors are likely to spot any number of interesting plants and animals.

The park has served a key role in bison restoration and today the giant beasts roam the park freely. It's not uncommon to encounter them in the most mundane of places such as the middle of the road, parking lots, or the lawn in front of your rental cabin. Give them plenty of room; it's their home.

Other large species easily found include moose, elk, deer, black bears, and coyotes. An assortment of small mammals also make regular appearances. Various species of ground squirrels and chipmunks hang out in picnic areas waiting for handouts (please don't). Grizzly bear and wolves can also be spotted but are less common. These species are more likely to be found by venturing a bit further from the main roads. A quiet drive at dusk is also a good way to spot animals such as fox, badger, and flying squirrels just as they are starting to become active. Birds put on a show almost anywhere you go in the park.

Bison Have Right of Way in Yellowstone

But what sets Yellowstone apart and captures the imagination is its geothermal activity. Sitting atop a massive caldera, Yellowstone is the largest active geyser field on the planet. In places within the caldera, the earth's crust is only a couple of miles thick. Groundwater seeps into crevices in the rocks and becomes superheated, creating a variety of hydro-thermal features. When heat, water, and pressure combine, fumaroles and geysers form, releasing steam and gas or shooting superheated water into the air. When the water is able to flow freely, hot springs and bubbling mudpots are formed. These often sport a wild array of vivid colors caused by bacterial growth, amazingly able to survive the extreme heat. Old Faithful may be the celebrity in the park, but Yellowstone has over 10,000 geothermal features. There are eight easily accessible geyser basins throughout the park, each with its own character and each well worth the travel time to visit.

Looking like ornate fountains out of a formal garden, the Travertine Terraces found at Mammoth Hot Springs at the northern end of the park are my favorites. Unlike their showy geyser cousins, the terraces have a graceful beauty. Hot water rises through limestone, dissolving carbonate in the rock along the way and carrying it to the surface. Carbon dioxide is released at the surface and calcium carbonate deposited as travertine. These natural fountains are constantly changing as new layers of travertine are deposited.

With its abundant wildlife, sweeping vistas, and otherworldly landscapes, Yellowstone is a place that feeds the soul and inspires the imagination.

Mammoth Hot Springs

THE RETURN OF WOLVES TO YELLOWSTONE

Throughout most of human history the big, bad wolf has been one of our greatest villains. Seen as depleters of game, destroyers of livestock, and killers of children, wolves have been mercilessly slaughtered wherever they come in contact with humans. Even in the national parks which carried a mandate to preserve wild animals, wolves were the exception. In the 1930s, in order to preserve the majestic herds of elk that tourists came to see, wolves were systematically extirpated from Yellowstone. For more than 50 years those elk (along with bison, deer, and other herbivores) roamed across the landscape largely unchecked.

In 1995, after a great deal of heated debate, a small pack of wolves was relocated from western Canada to Yellowstone. The pack thrived and soon, scientists discovered, so did the park! The return of the wolves triggered a cascade of events, starting with those herds of elk. Now at risk of being hunted by the wolves, the elk changed their grazing patterns. They moved out of the narrow stream and river valleys and into more open grazing land where there was less cover for wolves. This in turn relieved the grazing pressure on the stream and river banks and allowed native aspen and willow to grow back. Songbirds flourished and beavers returned, further transforming the landscape.

Sentiment for wolves seems split between two extremes. Either they are the things of nightmares, villains, and vicious predators, or they are seen as wise spirits of the natural world, possessing knowledge beyond that of man. The reality is that they are top predators in an ecosystem that maintains a delicate balance among all of its parts. Wolves are neither good nor bad in any human sense of the words. They are necessary. They have a role to play and it is for us to step aside and let them play it. Yellowstone has a stronger, more varied ecosystem because of the wolves that roam through it. And the fact that many humans find them to be beautiful creatures that instill a feeling of wild nobility? Well, let's call that an added bonus.

HOWL

Howl is a lacy stole that captures the essence of wolves in Yellowstone. The center panel with paw prints is knit flat, end to end. Stitches are then picked up around the sides and the border, filled with trees and snowflakes, is knit in the round.

SIZES
One Size

FINISHED MEASUREMENTS
Length 60 inches / 152.5 cm
Width 16 inches / 40.5 cm

MATERIALS
Yarn: Knit Picks Gloss Lace (70% merino wool, 30% silk; 440 yards/50 grams); color: Hawk; 2 skeins

Needles: 40 inch US #5 / 3.75 mm circular needle, or size needed to obtain gauge

Stitch markers
Tapestry needle

GAUGE
24 sts and 32 rows = 4 inches / 10 cm in stockinette stitch worked flat

PATTERN NOTES

The center panel of the stole is knit flat. Stitches are then picked up around the edges and the border is worked in the round.

You will be working two m1 increases in a row at the corners of the border. Lift the bar and knit into the back loop to create the first m1 and then simply repeat this for the second m1.

SPECIAL STITCHES AND TECHNIQUES

Cdd (central double decrease): Sl 2 sts together knitwise, k1, pass the 2 slipped stitches over the knit stitch.

Kyok (knit, yarn over, knit): Knit, then yo, then knit again into the the same st. Three sts made from 1 st.

Stretchy bind off: K2, place tip of LH needle into fronts of these 2 sts, k2tog, *k1, place tip of LH needle into fronts of these 2 sts, k2tog, rep from * until all sts have been bound off.

PATTERN

Center Panel (worked flat)
With a provisional cast on, CO 21 sts.
Work 23 reps of Chart 1.

Border (worked in the round)
Pick up knitwise 245 sts evenly from the left edge of the center panel (2 sts for every 3 rows), pm.
Open the provisional CO and pick up 21 sts, pm.
Pick up knitwise 245 sts evenly from the right edge of the center panel (2 sts for every 3 rows), pm.
Knit 21 sts, pm.
Work border charts as follows:
[One rep of Chart 2, four reps of Chart 3, one rep of Chart 4, slm, one rep of Chart 5, slm] twice.
Continue in pattern until all chart rows have been worked once.
BO all sts using the stretchy bind off.

Weave in loose ends.
Block flat taking care to form the points.

CHART 1

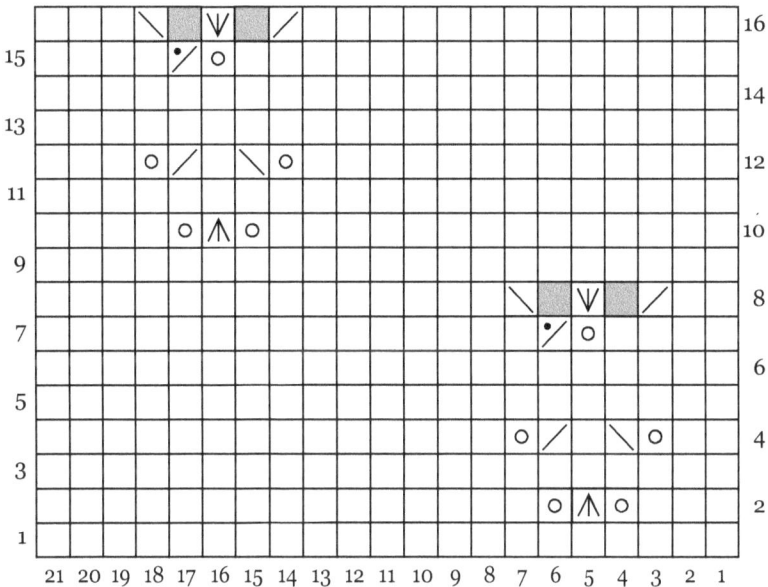

CHART KEY

▦ No stitch	⋁ Slip	⋁ Kyok	⁄ P2tog			
☐ Knit	○ Yarn over	⁄ K2tog	⋀ CDD			
• Purl	M Make 1	＼ Ssk				

Chart 2

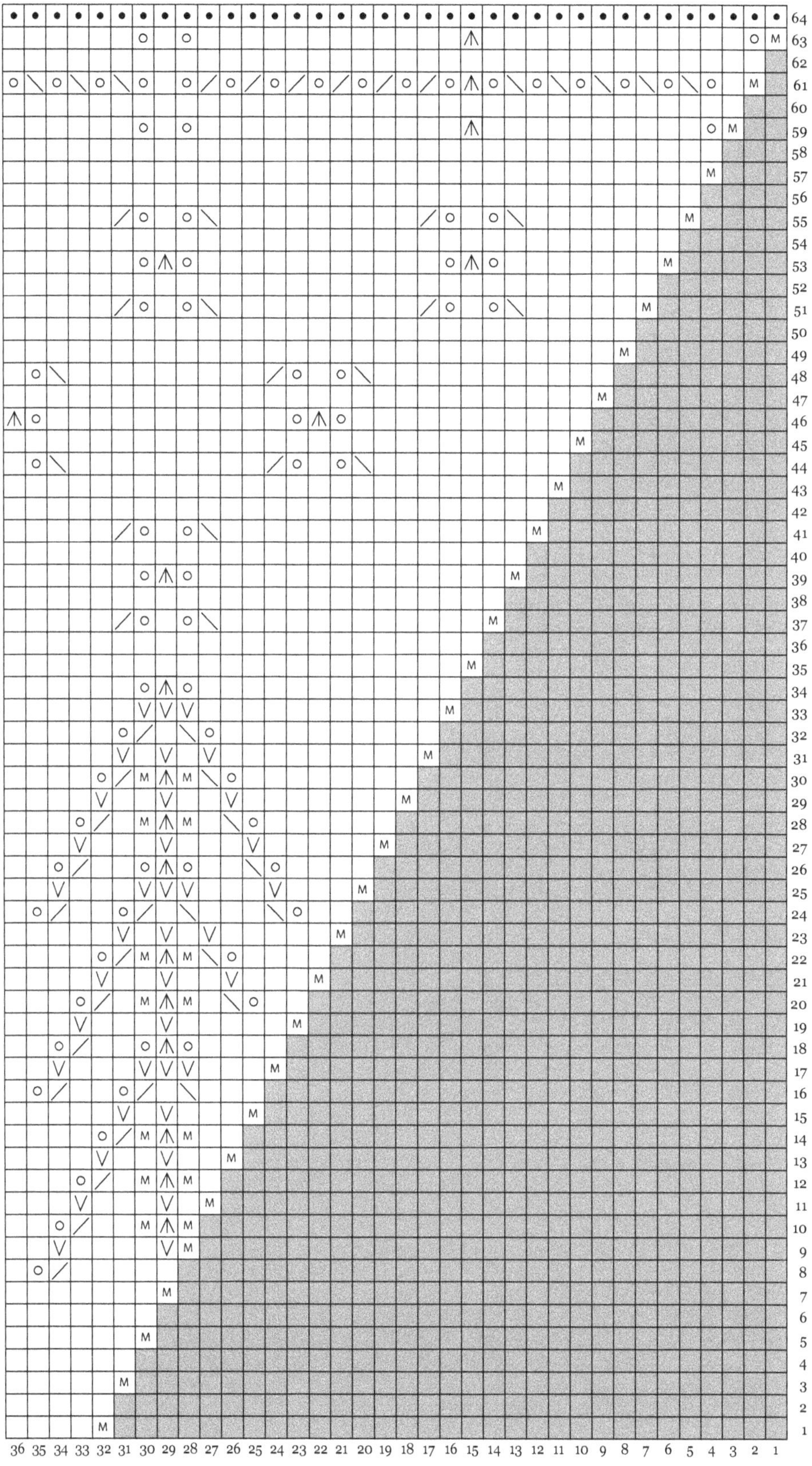
64 63 62 61 60 59 58 57 56 55 54 53 52 51 50 49 48 47 46 45 44 43 42 41 40 39 38 37 36 35 34 33 32 31 30 29 28 27 26 25 24 23 22 21 20 19 18 17 16 15 14 13 12 11 10 9 8 7 6 5 4 3 2 1
36 35 34 33 32 31 30 29 28 27 26 25 24 23 22 21 20 19 18 17 16 15 14 13 12 11 10 9 8 7 6 5 4 3 2 1

CHART 3

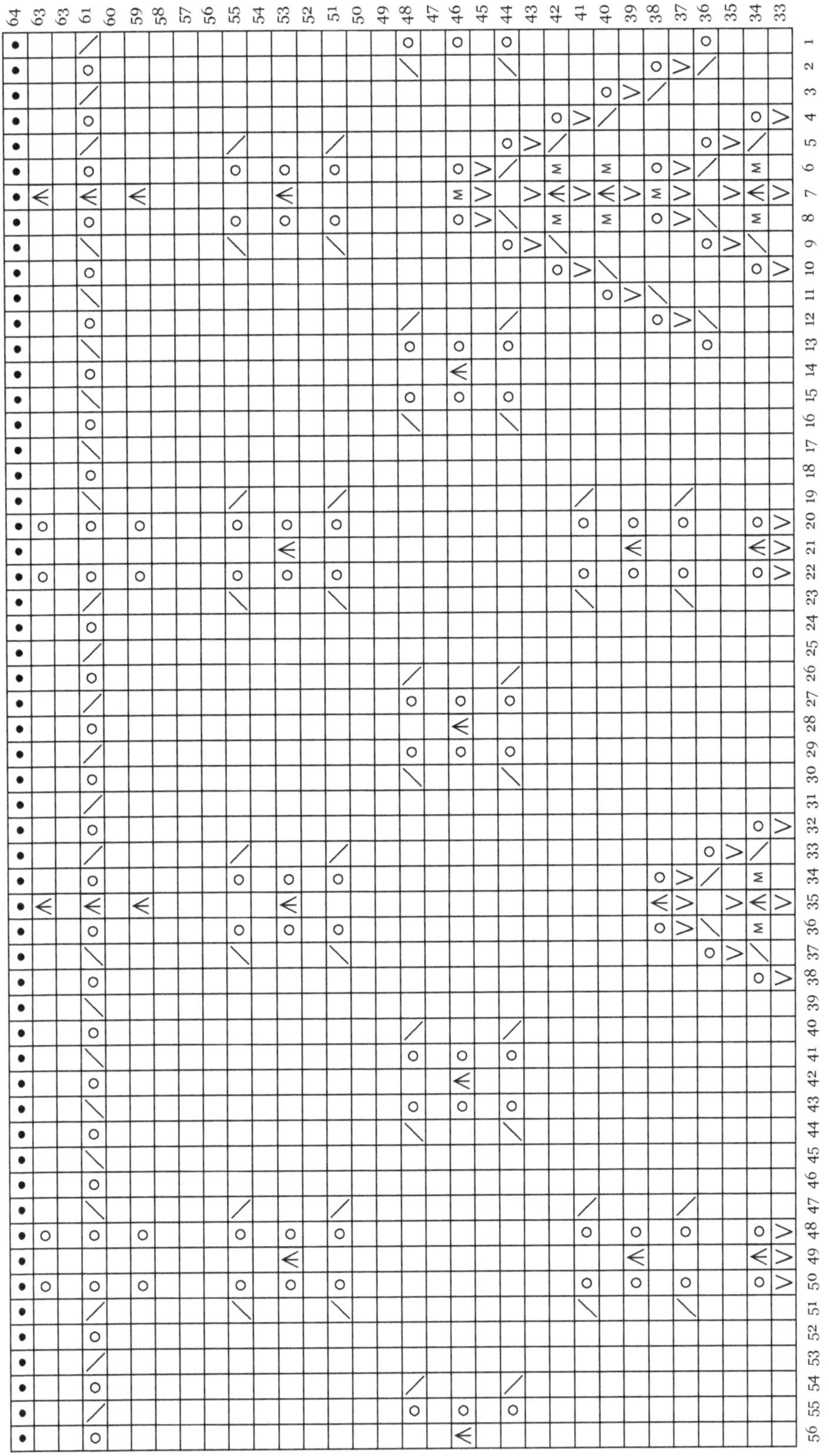

CHART 4

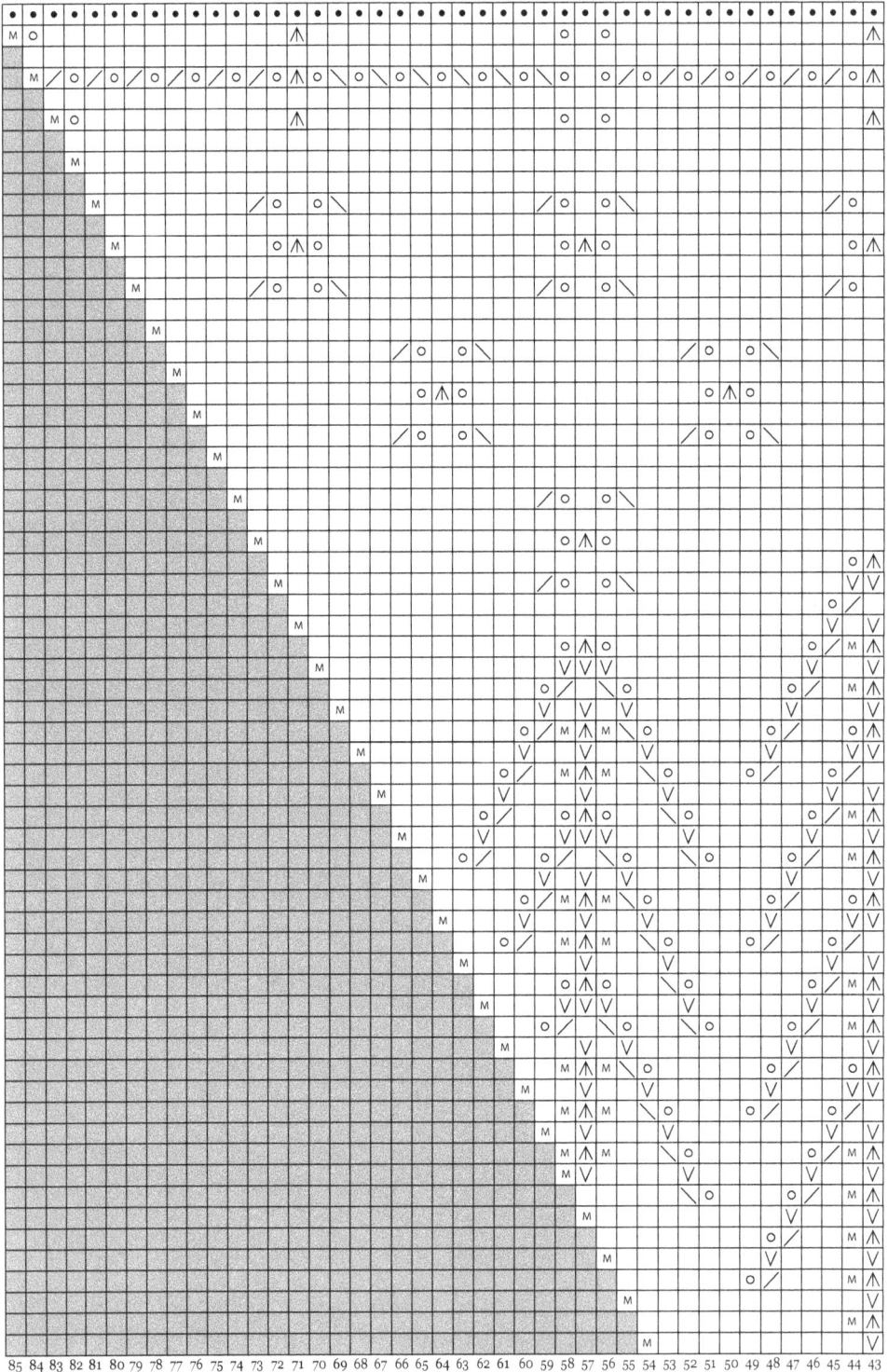

CHART 5

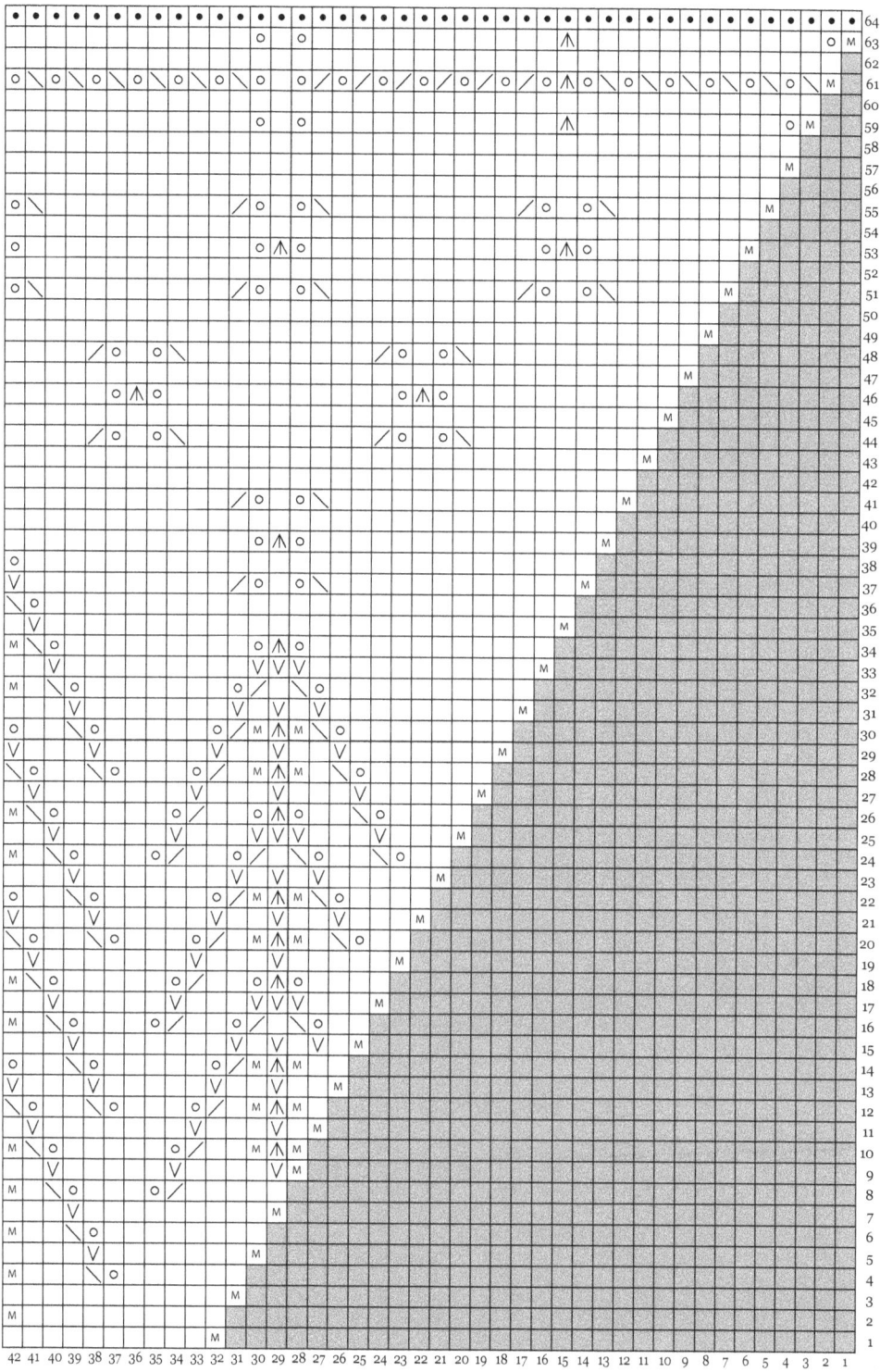

OLYMPIC NATIONAL PARK

Established in 1938 and encompassing almost a million acres, Olympic National Park protects what was described as "the finest sample of primeval forests of Sitka spruce, western hemlock, Douglas fir, and western red-cedar in the entire United States." Today, visitors can stand among these ancient giants in the moss-covered temperate rain forests of the park. Twelve to fourteen feet of yearly rainfall nourish the lush understory, which includes shrubs, ferns, and wildflowers. This diverse park also offers glacier-topped mountains, and miles and miles of wild Pacific coastline where visitors can hike, fish, and camp.

One of the gems of Olympic National Park is the delicate Pacific trillium, whose three petaled white flowers appear only briefly in the spring. It is a member of the genus *Trillium*, a group of flowering perennials with 39 species distributed throughout North America's temperate zones. Some species are common and can be found in backyard gardens, while others are highly endangered and found only in very specific areas.

Trilliums grow as rhizomes underground and in the spring send up stalks, called scapes, that each have a single flower. Trilliums produce no true leaves; however, the three green bracts below the flower are photo-synthetic and produce food for the plant. The single flower is composed of three petals and may be white, red, purple, pink, yellow, or green. The stalks will die back naturally in the heat of summer, but picking the stalk can kill the plant by depriving the rhizome below of food for the following year. If left undisturbed the plants are hardy and can live 25 years or more.

The trillium is a perfect symbol of the beauty of the natural world around us. These lovely flowers are a balance of strength and fragility that can be explored and admired, but ultimately, need to be left alone to flourish.

Crab Orchard Falls Trillium, Crab Orchard Falls Trail, NC
Photo: ©Knit Eco Chic by Lindsay Lewchuk

"Growing up in Ontario instilled in me a fascination for the Provincial flower, Trillium. Near our home in the North Carolina mountains, I discovered this shade loving plant thrives! While hiking up to a waterfall/knitwear photo shoot, my mom and I passed dozens of rich purple Trillium sprouting from the mounds of decaying leaves from seasons gone by. In the heart of the woodland, the lack of sunlight shining through the dense canopy caused the colour to shine vibrantly from the ground capturing my interest and enticing me to pause to take a photo (or dozen)."

TRILLIUM

Trillium is a close fitting hat with a lovely three-petaled lace design on the crown. It is knit from the top down and is finished with a pretty mossy rib brim.

SIZES
One Size

FINISHED MEASUREMENTS
Band circumference 19 inches / 48.25 cm (unstretched)

MATERIALS
Yarn: Knit Picks Wool of the Andes Worsted (100% wool; 110 yards/50 grams); color: Cloud; 1 skein

Needles: Set of 4 US #8 / 5 mm double pointed needles
Set of 4 US #6 / 4 mm double pointed needles, or size needed to obtain gauge

6 stitch markers
Tapestry needle

GAUGE
20 sts and 32 rnds = 4 inches / 10 cm in mossy rib with smaller needles

PATTERN NOTES

This hat is knit top down which means it starts with just a few cast-on stitches. An i-cord technique for the first row is used to help prevent twisting.

The pattern is written assuming you will use a set of 4 double pointed needles with the stitches evenly distributed on the 3 needles. If you prefer to use the magic loop method on a circular needle, you will need to add additional stitch markers to mark the breaks between needles.

SPECIAL STITCHES AND TECHNIQUES

Sk2p (slip, knit 2 together, pass slipped stitch over): Sl1 st knitwise, knit 2 sts together, pass the slipped st over.

STITCH PATTERNS

Mossy Rib
Rnds 1 and 2: *K2, p1, k1, p2; rep from * to end of rnd.
Rnds 3 and 4: *K1, p1, k2, p2; rep from * to end of rnd.
Rep rnds 1 - 4 for pattern.

THE PATTERN

Crown
With larger needles CO 6 sts onto one needle.
Rnd 1: Starting with the first cast on stitch and bringing the working yarn across the back as for an i-cord, knit

2 sts onto the first dpn, switch to the second dpn and knit 2 sts, switch to the third dpn and knit the last 2 sts.

Rnd 2: *M1, k1; rep from * to end of rnd. - 12 sts

Rnd 3 and all odd rnds: Knit all sts.

Rnd 4: [Yo, k1, yo, k3] three times. - 18 sts

Rnd 6: [Yo, k3, yo, k3] three times. - 24 sts

Rnd 8: [Yo, k5, yo, k3] three times. - 30 sts

Rnd 10: [Yo, k7, yo, m1, sk2p, m1] three times. - 36 sts

Rnd 12: [K1, yo, k7, yo, k4] three times. - 42 sts

Rnd 14: [K2, yo, k7, yo, k5] three times. - 48 sts

Rnd 16: [K3, yo, k7, yo, k6] three times. - 54 sts

Rnd 18: [K3, m1, k1, yo, ssk, k3, k2tog, yo, k1, m1, k6] three times. - 60 sts

Rnd 20: [K5, m1, k1, yo, ssk, k1, k2tog, yo, k1, m1, k8] three times. - 66 sts

Rnd 22: [K7, m1, k1, pm, yo, sk2p, yo, pm, k1, m1, k10] three times. - 72 sts

Rnd 24: [Knit to 2 sts before the marker, k2tog, slm, yo, k1, m1, knit to 1 sts before marker, m1, k1, yo, slm, ssk, knit to end of needle] three times. - 78 sts

Continue to work Rnd 24, alternating with knit rnds, until there are 108 sts.

Rnd 26: [Knit to 2 sts before the marker, k2tog, slm, yo, knit to marker, yo, slm, ssk, knit to end of needle] three times.

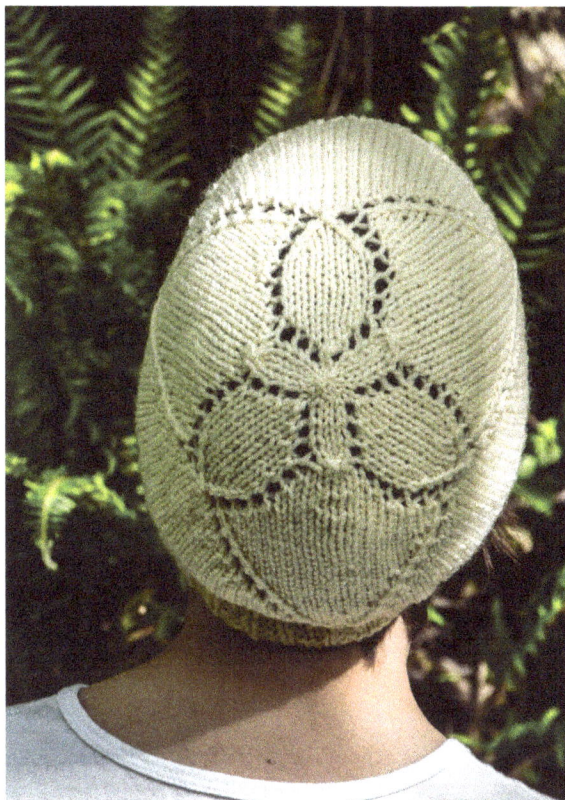

Continue to work rnd 26, alternating with knit rnds until only 1 st remains before the first marker on each needle.

Sl the first st on each needle so that it becomes the last st on the previous needle, removing the first marker from each needle.

Rnd 28: [Yo, knit to marker, yo, slm, ssk, k1, k2tog] three times.

Rnd 30: [Yo, knit to marker, yo, slm, sk2p] three times.

Knit one more rnd.

Switch to smaller needles and work 2 inches / 5 cm in mossy rib.

BO all sts.

Weave in loose ends.

Block gently.

SHENANDOAH NATIONAL PARK

Shenandoah National Park was established in 1935 as part of a push to expand the park system into the eastern United States. The park protects nearly 80,000 acres of mostly forested land in the Blue Ridge Mountains of Virginia, and is home to over 1400 species of plants as well as the numerous animals they sustain. The park, located only 75 miles from Washington DC, offers visitors an escape from urban life with ample opportunities to hike, camp, view wildlife, and relax in quiet seclusion. In the fall the changing leaves paint the hills in bright shades of crimson, orange, and yellow.

Starting in 1940, Shenandoah National Park has offered researchers an unusual, close up opportunity to study forest succession on a large scale. When the first surveys were performed, sections of the park still showed significant signs of having been cleared and cultivated by the people living in the area before the park formation. Over the past seven decades researchers have been able to observe and record the sequence of transitions as various tree species, one after another, filled in the open land. Today, the park is over 95% forested. The ridge tops are dominated by chestnut and red oak, which give way to areas of mixed hardwood forests, including maple, birch, ash, and basswood on the mid-slopes. Along the streams and lower slopes, yellow poplar forests thrive. The park continues to serve as a laboratory for researchers to study the effects of fire, storms, insect infestations, and disease outbreaks, as well as human activities, including climate disruption, on the ever-changing forest ecosystem.

Fall Foliage in East Greenbush; Photo: ©Gregory Polyakov
"This photo was taken in my own yard in the Hudson Valley Region of Upstate New York."

DECIDUOUS

Deciduous is a lovely fingerless mitt with a gusset thumb and a flared cuff. The hand is decorated with a broken rib pattern and the cuff has a lacy leaf motif.

SIZES
One Size

FINISHED MEASUREMENTS
Hand circumference 6 inches / 15.25 cm (unstretched)

MATERIALS
Yarn: Knit Picks Gloss DK (70% merino wool, 30% silk; 123 yards/50 grams); color: Clover; 1 skein

Needles: Set of 5 US #5 / 3.75 mm double pointed needles, or size needed to obtain gauge

Stitch holder or scrap yarn
Tapestry Needle

GAUGE
20 sts and 28 rnds = 4 inches / 10 cm in stockinette

SPECIAL STITCHES AND TECHNIQUES

Cdd (central double decrease): Sl 2 sts together knitwise, k1, pass the 2 slipped stitches over the knit stitch.

Stretchy bind off: K2, place tip of LH needle into fronts of these 2 sts, k2tog, *k1, place tip of LH needle into fronts of these 2 sts, k2tog, rep from * until all sts have been bound off.

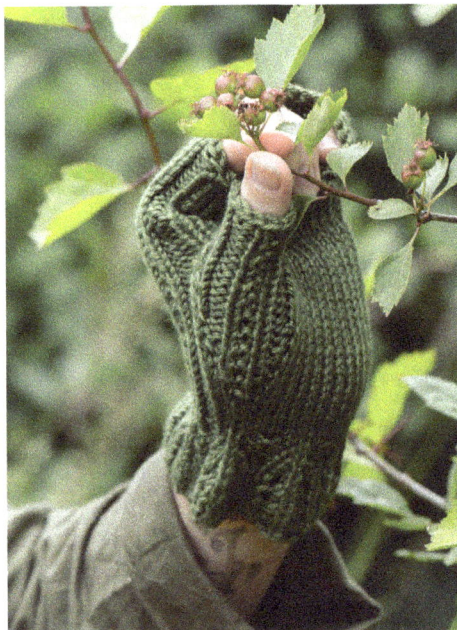

STITCH PATTERNS

Beaded Rib
Rnd 1: *P2, k3; rep from *.
Rnd 2: *P2, k1, p1, k1; rep from *.
Rep rnds 1 and 2 for pattern.

PATTERN

Cuff (Both Hands)
CO 35 sts and join in the round, taking care not to twist the work.
Rnd 1: *P2, k1, yo, k1, yo, k1; rep from * to end of rnd.
Rnd 2: *P2, k5; rep from * to end of rnd.
Rnd 3: *P2, k1, yo, k3, yo, k1; rep from * to end of rnd.

Rnd 4: *P2, k7; rep from * to end of rnd.
Rnd 5: *P2, k1, yo, ssk, k1, k2tog, yo, k1; rep from * to end of rnd.
Rnd 6: *P2, k7; rep from * to end of rnd.
Rnd 7: *P2, k1, yo, ssk, k1, k2tog, yo, k1; rep from * to end of rnd.
Rnd 8: *P2, k7; rep from * to end of rnd.
Rnd 9: *P2, k2, cdd, k2; rep from * to end of rnd.
Rnd 10: *P2, k5; rep from * to end of rnd.
Rnd 11: *P2, k1, cdd, k1; rep from * to end of rnd.
Rnd 12: *P2, k3; rep from * to end of rnd.
Rnd 13: *P2, m1, cdd, m1; rep from * to end of rnd.
Rnd 14: [P2, k3] four times, p2, k13.
Rnd 15: [P2, k1, p1, k1] four times, p2, k13.
Rep rnds 14 and 15 one more time.

Gusset (Left)
Work the first 20 sts in beaded rib, p2, k11, and work the remaining sts of each rnd as follows:
Rnd 16: M1, k1, m1, k1.
Rnd 17: K1, p1, k2.
Rnd 18: K4.
Rnd 19: M1, k1, p1, k1, m1, k1.
Rnd 20: P1, k3, p1, k1.

Rnd 21: P1, k1, p1, k1, p1, k1.
Rnd 22: M1, p1, k3, p1, m1, k1.
Rnd 23: P2, k1, p1, k1, p2, k1.
Rnd 24: P2, k3, p2, k1.
Rnd 25: M1, p2, k1, p1, k1, p2, m1, k1.
Rnd 26: K1, p2, k3, p2, k2.
Rnd 27: K1, p2, k1, p1, k1, p2, k2.
Rnd 28: M1,k1, p2, k3, p2, k1, m1, k1.
Rnd 29: K2, p2, k1, p1, k1, p2, k3.
Rnd 30: K2, p2, k3, p2, k3.

Gusset (Right)
Work the first 20 sts in beaded rib, p2, k1, work the next sts as follows, and knit the last 11 sts of each rnd.
Rnd 16: M1, k1, m1.
Rnd 17: K1, p1, k1.
Rnd 18: K3.
Rnd 19: M1, k1, p1, k1, m1.
Rnd 20: P1, k3, p1.
Rnd 21: P1, k1, p1, k1, p1.
Rnd 22: M1, p1, k3, p1, m1.
Rnd 23: P2, k1, p1, k1, p2.
Rnd 24: P2, k3, p2.
Rnd 25: M1, p2, k1, p1, k1, p2, m1.
Rnd 26: K1,p2, k3, p2, k1.
Rnd 27: K1, p2, k1, p1, k1, p2, k1.
Rnd 28: M1,k1, p2, k3, p2, k1, m1.
Rnd 29: K2, p2, k1, p1, k1, p2, k2.
Rnd 30: K2, p2, k3, p2, k2.

Hand (Left)
Work the first 20 sts in beaded rib, p2, k11, using the backward loop method, CO 2 sts, place the next 11 sts on scrap yarn, k1.
Continue working the first 20 sts in beaded rib, p2, k14, until the hand is 3 inches / 7.75 cm tall (or desired hand height).

BO all sts using the stretchy bind off.

Hand (Right)
Work the first 20 sts in beaded rib, p2, k1, using the backward loop method, CO 2 sts, place the next 11 sts on scrap yarn, k11.
Continue working the first 20 sts in beaded rib, p2, k14, until the hand is 3 inches / 7.75 cm tall (or desired hand height.)
BO all sts using the stretchy bind off.

Thumb (Both Hands)
Place 11 sts from the scrap yarn onto needles. Pick up 2 sts from the CO edge at the hand.
Rnd 1: K2, p2, k1, p1, k1, p2, k4.
Rnd 2: K2, p2, k3, p2, k4.
Rep rnds 1 and 2 until thumb is 1 inch / 2.5 cm tall (or desired thumb height.)
BO all sts using the stretchy bind off.

Weave in loose ends.
Block gently, taking care to shape the leaves.

Cuyahoga Valley National Park

With its twists, turns, and oxbows, the Cuyahoga River is the backbone of the Cuyahoga Valley National Park. Located just 20 miles outside of Cleveland, this park is a great example of what can happen when communities come together with a common purpose to preserve both natural and cultural heritage. Restored wetlands and reclaimed farmland are now home to a wide variety of plant and animal species. Many of the features of the park were shaped by human activity, and the park strives to preserve the human history of the land while also keeping a commitment to providing open space for wildlife to thrive.

The Ohio and Erie Canal, completed in 1833, connected Lake Erie with the Ohio River and was the last link in the larger canal system that connected the Great Lakes to the Mississippi River. For the next 30 years the canal was a busy thoroughfare for mule-drawn barges, allowing farms and businesses to move goods to market quickly and cheaply. The area flourished and Ohio became the third most prosperous state in the country. However, by the late 1800s most goods were transported by trains, and the canal was only used by recreational boaters and as a water source for industry. By 1913, the canal was completely abandoned.

In the early 1990s, as the surrounding cities grew, visitors began to use the Cuyahoga Valley for recreation. Fearing urban sprawl, civic groups formed and spearheaded a movement to preserve and reclaim the landscape for recreational use. The creation of Cuyahoga Valley National Park included a mixture of historical preservation, habitat restoration, and toxic waste clean-up. Today the old canal towpath serves as the main trail through the park. Visitors can walk through forests, field, and wetlands, as well as explore sites of historical and cultural interest.

Twin Sisters Falls in Cuyahoga Valley National Park; Photo: @ Meri Ruble

"The waterfall image was captured on a bitter cold day just after New Years 2018, at Twin Sisters Falls in Cuyahoga Valley National Park. A friend and I bundled up and hiked the frozen creek and discovered layers of textured ice, fed from groundwater above, trickling over the layers of sedimentary shale formed from ancient seas. The dual falls is beautiful year round, but in the cold drab winter it becomes like a gemstone, nuanced and faceted with blues and greens, yellows and whites."

Cuyahoga Canals

Cuyahoga Canals is a close fitting hat with unusual construction. Two bands are knit flat, then twisted around each other and joined in the round. The neat parallel rows created by the twisted rib pattern highlight the curves created with blocking. Stitches are picked up along the edge of the band and the top of the hat is completed.

Sizes
Small (Large)
Sample shown is large

Finished Measurements
Band Circumference 20 (22) inches / 50.75 (55.75) cm (unstretched)

Materials
Yarn: Knit Picks Wool of the Andes Worsted (100% wool; 110 yards/50 grams); color: Fern; 2 skeins

Needles: 32 inch US #8 / 5mm circular needle, or size needed to obtain gauge
Set of 5 US #8 / 5 mm double pointed needles, or size needed to obtain gauge

Tapestry needle

Gauge
18 sts and 26 rnds = 4 inches / 10 cm in stockinette stitch

PATTERN NOTES

As written you will work both bands at the same time. If you prefer, you can work them individually.

STITCH PATTERNS

Half Twisted Rib

Row 1 (WS): Sl1, *k1, p1; rep from * to last st, k1.
Row 2 (RS): Sl1, *k1tbl, p1; rep from * to last st, k1tbl.
Rep rows 1 and 2 for pattern.

PATTERN

Band

With 1 skein, CO 20 sts and with the second skein, CO 20 sts onto the same needle.
Work the following for each band taking care to keep the skeins separate.

Work half twisted rib pattern until the bands are 20 (22) inches / 50.75 (55.75) cm long.
BO all sts.

Weave the 2 pieces around each other as shown in the photo and block flat. Be sure the pieces cross

each other 4 times.
Sew the ends together to form a tube.

Crown
Rnd 1: Using 4 dpns, pick up 84 (92) sts evenly along one edge of the tube. Be sure there are 21 (23) sts per needle.
Rnd 2: Knit.
Rnd 3: Knit.
Rnd 4: [Ssk, knit to last 2 sts before end of needle, k2tog] four times. - 8 sts decreased
Rnd 5: Knit.
Rnd 6: Knit.
Rep rnds 4 - 6 until there are 52 (60) sts remaining.

Rep rnds 4 and 5 until there are 12 sts remaining.

FINISHING
Cut yarn leaving an 8 inch / 20.25 cm tail. With the tapestry needle, thread the tail through the remaining sts, slipping them off the needle. Pull tight to close the top of the hat.

Weave in loose ends.
Block to shape. You may wish to use a spray bottle and only wet the sections of the hat that need shaping to avoid removing the graceful curves of the band formed during the previous blocking step.

HATS, FEATHERS, AND THE MIGRATORY BIRD TREATY ACT

In the late 1800s and early 1900s it was fashionable for women's hats to be decorated with masses of colorful feathers or even entire stuffed birds. This booming feather trade decimated many bird populations. Labrador ducks, great auks, passenger pigeons, Carolina parakeets, and heath hens were hunted to extinction and numerous other species were on the brink. The American Ornithologist Union (AOU), an early conservation group, advocated for the protection of birds hunted for the feather trade, as well as birds affected by "eggers" who harvested eggs by the hundreds for egg collectors. The AOU established the Committee on the Protection of North American Birds to push for stronger laws backed by fines. Prominent AOU member and sportsman Dr George Bird Grinnell created the first Audubon Society in 1886 for the protection of wild birds and their eggs. This group quickly attracted tens of thousands of members and then collapsed. However, the seed was planted, and in 1896 the Massachusetts Audubon Society was formed. By the turn of the century, a quarter of US states had Audubon Societies advocating for the protection of wild birds.

One of the biggest impediments to bird conservation is the fact that they move around, some migrating enormous distances each year. Birds that might have been protected under one state's laws could legally be hunted under another's. In 1913, Congress passed the Weeks-McLean Migratory Bird Act, which banned the spring shooting of migratory game and insectivorous birds, placing them under the "custody and protection" of the federal government. Two district courts quickly ruled that the act violated states' rights because it was outside the scope of what the federal government was constitutionally allowed to do.

However, the Constitution does grant the federal government the unequivocal authority to make treaties. In 1916, the US signed a treaty with Great Britain (on the behalf of Canada, then part of the British Empire), agreeing to stop all hunting of insectivorous birds and to establish specific hunting seasons for game birds. In order to implement the treaty,

Congress passed the Migratory Bird Treaty Act (MBTA) in 1918, which officially made it a crime to "pursue, hunt, take, capture, kill," or "sell" a migratory bird or any of its parts, including nests, eggs, and feathers. In 1920 the Supreme Court upheld the act, ruling that it did not violate states' rights. Since then, treaties have been signed with Mexico, Japan, and the Soviet Union (now Russia) resulting in the protection of nearly all wild birds within the United States.

Over time, as the threats to bird populations have changed, so has the enforcement of the MBTA. In the 1970s, US prosecutors began charging oil and gas, timber, mining, chemical, and electricity companies with incidentally killing protected birds, if those deaths could have been prevented with simple infrastructure or procedure changes. Under the concept of "incidental take," BP was required to pay $100 million in criminal fines for the Deepwater Horizon oil spill that killed more than a million birds. In addition to being held responsible for catastrophic events, companies were required to use best practices to prevent bird deaths whenever possible and could be fined for failure to use these measures.

In December of 2017, nearly a hundred years after the passage of the Migratory Bird Treaty Act, the federal government chose to significantly weaken the law by reducing its scope of enforcement. The Department of the Interior under Ryan Zinke issued a memo stating that the MBTA does not prohibit the incidental take of migratory birds. This means that companies whose activities result in avoidable incidental bird deaths will no longer be liable for those deaths, as long as the purpose of the activity is not to kill birds. This puts millions of additional birds at peril as companies will no longer be required to even attempt to mitigate bird deaths.

The National Audubon Society is once again in the middle of the fight to protect wild birds. In May 2018, they filed a lawsuit in federal court against the Department of the Interior. Consider joining the National Audubon Society or your local Audubon Society and adding your voice to the fight.

ARANSAS NATIONAL WILDLIFE REFUGE

Aransas National Wildlife Refuge, located on the east coast of Texas, was established in 1937 as a refuge and breeding ground for migratory birds and other wildlife. A long chain of barrier islands just off the coast protects a series of shallow bays and marshes. The saltmarsh habitat that straddles land and sea contains salt-tolerant plants which diminish the effects of waves and tides, filter pollutants, and provide habitat for hermit crabs and other marine invertebrates. Further inland, where the saltwater mixes with fresh, there are nurseries for young fish. These brackish waters teem with blue crab and other shellfish. Away from the influence of the saltwater, the freshwater marshes provide a home to alligators, turtles, frogs, snakes and many other wildlife species. This highly varied landscape provides an abundance of food which attracts over 400 species of birds. The refuge is the winter home of the last wild flock of whooping cranes.

Whooping cranes are one of just two species of cranes in North America. Adult birds are all white with a vivid red cap. They stand nearly five feet tall and have a seven and a half foot wingspan. These large, majestic birds with their snowy white feathers were much prized by the feather trade. By 1941 the crane population had been reduced to just 21 wild birds and 2 more in captivity. People needed to take action if the species was to survive. In 1967, the whooping crane was added to the endangered species list, and conservation groups began working both to protect the remaining wild birds and to breed birds in captivity.

The last wild breeding population of whooping cranes spends its summers at Wood Buffalo National Park in Canada and then migrates 2,400 miles through the heart of the US to the Aransas National Wildlife Refuge, making stops at prairies and wetlands along the way to rest and feed. Thanks to conservation efforts, the total population of this flock has grown to over 300 individuals. With as many as 80 breeding pairs, the flock is considered self-sustaining. However, they are still extremely vulnerable to major events in their environment such as wildfires or oil spills.

Researchers have established two additional flocks of whooping cranes through captive breeding programs. One is a non-migratory group living at Kissimmee Prairie in Florida. The second effort created an eastern migratory population. The Whooping Crane Eastern Partnership raised whooping crane chicks on the Necedah National Wildlife Refuge in Wisconsin. They then guided them to Florida's Chassahowitzka National Wildlife Refuge, using ultra-light aircraft to teach the birds the migration route. The sight of a string of young cranes trailing behind the wing of an ultralight airplane has become one of the most enduring and endearing images of the whooping crane's story.

While these and other recent efforts have been successful in increasing the population size and range of the whooping cranes, they remain one of the rarest birds in North America and continue to need our protection and assistance. In 2017, in a clear signal of changing priorities, the federal government abruptly cut funding for the Patuxent Wildlife Research Center's whooping crane conservation program, ending their 51 years of successfully breeding and training whooping cranes for release.

October 2, 2012: Five endangered whooping cranes learn their new migration route in Marquette County, WI; Photo: Operation Migration. U.S. Fish and Wildlife Service Southeast Region

WHOOP! WHOOP!

Whoop! Whoop! is a close fitting cloche with a lovely chevron pattern encircling the brim. The hat starts at the crown using a continuous cast-on. The lace brim is worked sideways and knitted on to the rest of the hat.

SIZES
Small (Large)
Sample shown is small

FINISHED MEASUREMENTS
Band circumference 19 (22) inches / 48.25 (55.75) cm (unstretched)

MATERIALS
Yarn: Knit Picks Chroma Twist Bulky (70% superwash wool, 30% nylon; 127 yards/100 grams); color: Red Velvet; 1 skein

Needles: 40 inch US #8 / 5 mm circular needle, or size needed to obtain gauge
US #8 / 5 mm straight needles, or size needed to obtain gauge

Tapestry needle

GAUGE
16 sts and 24 rnds = 4 inches / 10 cm in stockinette stitch

PATTERN NOTES

This pattern assumes that you are familiar with "Judy's Magic Cast On" and "magic loop" techniques.

SPECIAL STITCHES AND TECHNIQUES

Cdd (central double decrease): Sl 2 sts together knitwise, k1, pass the 2 slipped stitches over the knit stitch.

THE PATTERN:

Crown

Using Judy's Magic Cast On CO 36st onto a 40 inch circular needle (18 sts per side.)

Rnd 1: Knit.

Rnd 2: [K1, m1, knit to last st of the side, m1, k1] twice. - 4 sts increased

Rep rnds 1 and 2 until there are 84

(92) stitches

Knit 8 rounds even.

Clip yarn leaving a tail and set the crown section aside

Brim

(Starting with the plume decoration)

On the straight needles, CO 21 st.

Row 1 (WS): Knit.
Row 2 (RS): kfb, k8, cdd, k8, kfb,
Row 3: K1, p19, k1.
Rep rows 2 and 3 two more times
(three reps total)
Row 4: Kfb, k1, ssk, k2, ssk, k1, cdd,
k1, k2tog, k2, k2tog, k1, kfb.
Row 5: K1, p15, k1.
Row 6: Kfb, ssk, ssk, ssk, cdd, k2tog,
k2tog, k2tog, kfb.
Row 7: K1, p9, k1.

Join the brim to the crown
Using the right hand needle of the
cir. needle holding the crown, work
the brim stitches from the straight
needle.
Row 8 (RS): Kfb, k3, cdd, k3, kfb.
Continue working flat.
Row 9 (WS): K1, p9, k2tog, p1, pass
the knit stitch over the purl stitch,
turn the work.
Rep rows 8 and 9 until all the crown
stitches have been worked.
Row 10: Knit.
Row 11: K1, p9, k1.
BO all sts.

FINISHING
With the tail from the bind off, sew
the bound off edge to the underside
of the beginning of the brim band.

Tack the plume decoration in place.

Weave in any remaining loose ends.

Block well to shape. A display head
or rolled up towels will help with
this.

Midway Atoll National Wildlife Refuge

Midway Atoll was claimed for the US in 1867. In 1903, the Pacific Cable Company sent workers as part of an effort to lay a trans-Pacific telegraph cable. That same year the Navy created a radio station there to deter squatters and poachers. Between 1904 and 1908 President Roosevelt stationed Marines on the island to prevent destruction of the abundant wildlife and to protect the cable workers. A brief tourist trade flourished between 1935 and 1941. Guests arrived in Flying Clippers (Martin M-130 flying boats) and were transported to the "Gooneyville Lodge." The lodge was named for the albatrosses, affectionately called "gooney birds," that populated the island.

With the start of World War II, the Navy significantly expanded its presence on the island, creating the Naval Air Facility Midway Island. The population on the island swelled and significant infrastructure was built. The facility continued to operate through the Cold War. However, its importance diminished and in 1988 the Midway Atoll National Wildlife Refuge was overlaid on the base. In 1993, the base was closed completely. Today the island retains its dual heritage both as a vital marine refuge and as an important historic site.

Located at the extreme northern end of the Hawaiian archipelago, Midway Atoll is made up of an elliptical outer reef nearly five miles in diameter surrounding 580,392 acres of ocean and submerged reef as well as three flat coral islands totaling approximately 1,549 acres. The atoll is the primary nesting ground for three species of albatrosses including the endangered short-tailed albatross. Boobies, frigatebirds, petrols, sheer-waters, and others (20 species in all) also nest on the island, covering virtually every inch and creating a cacophony that gives the island its Hawaiian name, "Pihemanu," meaning "the loud din of birds." The crystal waters of the lagoon teem with life, hosting a complex coral reef community of over 250 species. Spinner dolphins and green sea turtles frequent the lagoon. A small population of highly endangered Hawaiian monk seals also call the island home.

Despite living on a remote island, the animals that call Midway home are not free from the effects of human activity. Every day plastic debris from The Great Pacific Garbage Patch washes up on the atoll's beaches, where albatross parents unwittingly feed it to their chicks. Studies of Laysan Albatrosses suggest that nearly all of the individuals on the island have some plastic in their digestive systems and that one third of chicks die from ingesting plastic. Sea turtles, monk seals, and a wide variety of other species are also known to mistake plastic for food. The good news is that ocean cleanup efforts are underway, but it remains to be seen how effective current technology will be in accomplishing the task. Using reusable grocery sacks, choosing products with less packaging, and taking the time to properly recycle the plastic we do use are just a few of the small measures we can take at home to help mitigate this growing problem.

Laysan Albatross Courtship Dance
Midway Atoll National Wildlife Refuge March 2012
Photo: Noah Kahn/USFWS

PIHEMANU

Pihemanu is a crescent-shaped shawlette knit from end to end. The shape is created by binding off stitches at the beginning of each row and adding them back in strategically across the row. The color changes (worked as intarsia) align with the increase lines and emphasize the changes in stitch direction forming a lovely swirl pattern. As the piece grows it will continue to curl around on itself, creating a shawlette that securely hugs the shoulders.

SIZES
One Size

FINISHED MEASUREMENTS
Length 62 inches / 157.5 cm
Width 9 inches / 22.75 cm

MATERIALS
Yarn: Knit Picks Gloss DK (70% merino wool, 30% silk; 123 yards/50 grams); color A: Winter Night, 2 skeins; color B: Kenai, 1 skein; color C: Tranquil, 1 skein

Needles: US #8 / 5mm straight needles, or size needed to obtain gauge

Stitch markers
Tapestry needle

GAUGE
18 sts and 24 rows = 4 inches in stockinette stitch

Pattern Notes

At each color transition be sure to wrap the yarns to prevent holes in the work.

Pattern

Set-Up
With color A, CO 2 sts.
Row 1 (RS): [Kfb] twice. - 4 sts
Row 2 (WS): Knit.
Row 3: [Kfb] four times. - 8 sts
Row 4: Knit.
Row 5: *K1, kfb; rep from * to end of row. - 12 sts
Row 6: K5, pm, k5, pm, k1, pm, k1.
Row 7: Color A: kfb, slm, kfb, slm, Color B: k4, kfb, slm, Color C: k4, kfb. - 16 sts
Row 8: Color C: k3, p3, slm, Color B: p6, Color A: p1, k1, slm, k2.
Row 9: Color A: knit to marker, m1, slm, knit to 1 st before marker, kfb, slm, Color B: knit to 1 st before marker, kfb, slm, Color C: knit to last 4 sts, kfb, k3. - 4 sts incr
Row 10: K4, purl to last 4 sts switching colors in the same places as the previous row, k4.
Rep rows 9 and 10 until you have 56 sts.
Row 11: Color A: knit to marker, m1, slm, knit to 1 st before marker, kfb, slm, Color B: knit to 1 st before marker, kfb, slm, Color C: knit to last 4 sts, kfb, k3. - 4 sts incr
Row 12: (Remove markers as you go) k4, purl to last 8 sts switching colors in the same places as the previous row, k8.

Body
Row 13: Color A: BO4, m1, k11, m1, k11, m1, Color B: k15, kfb, Color C: k17.
Row 14 and all even rows: K4, purl to last 8 sts switching colors in the same places as the previous row, k8.

Rep rows 13 and 14 until the piece is 44" long measured along the outside edge of color C.

Finish

Row 15: Color A: BO4, k23, Color B: k16, Color C: k16.
Row 16 and all even rows: K4, purl to last 8 sts switching colors in the same places as the previous row, k8.
Row 17: Color A: BO4, k21, Color B: k15, Color C: k15.
Row 19: Color A: BO4, k19, Color B: k14, Color C: k14.
Row 21: Color A: BO4, k17, Color B: k13, Color C: k13.
Row 23: Color A: BO4, k15, Color B: k12, Color C: k12.
Rwo 25: Color A: BO4, k13, Color B: k11, Color C: k11.
Row 27: Color A: BO4, k11, Color B: k10, Color C: k10.
Row 29: Color A: BO4, k9, Color B: k9, Color C: k9.
Row 31: Color A: BO4, k7, Color B: k8, Color C: k8.
Row 33: Color A: BO4, k5, Color B: k7, Color C: k7.
Row 35: Color A: BO4, k3, Color B: k6, Color C: k6.
Row 36: K4, p4, k8, switching colors in the same places as the previous row.
Cut colors B and C, continue with color A only.
Row 37: BO4, knit to end of row.
Row 38: Knit.
Rep rows 37 and 38 two more times (three reps total.)
BO 4 sts.

Weave in loose ends.
Block gently, taking care to form curved shape.

DELTA NATIONAL WILDLIFE REFUGE

Delta National Wildlife Refuge was established in 1935 and protects 49,000 acres of Mississippi River delta in Louisiana. The refuge is an ever shifting landscape of marshes, bogs, bayous, sandbars, and small islands surrounded by water rich in fish, shellfish, and other invertebrates.

The area protected by the Delta National Wildlife Refuge was formed in the mid-1800 when the Mississippi River broke through its banks, depositing large quantities of silt, and creating new land called a deltaic splay. Since then, the water has continued to flow over this land, slowly eroding it away in some places while depositing yet more silt in other places, resulting in an unpredictable landscape. Humans have attempted to disrupt this cycle of flooding and erosion by building levees. While the levees have proved successful in preventing flood damage, they also cut off the wetlands from their supply of fresh water and sand that are required to replenish the landscape and maintain the habitat for the creatures that live there.

This ever-changing landscape hosts an equally fluid array of birds. Tens of thousands of waterfowl and shorebirds spent their winters on the refuge. In the spring and fall the bird population swells as migrating birds take a much needed stop to feed and rest before continuing their journeys. In the summer, nesting species, including the exotic looking roseate spoonbill, mate and rear young. The refuge also provides a year round home for numerous mammal, amphibian, and reptile species including the endangered American alligator.

Black-Crowned Night Heron. This is one of the many species protected by the Migratory Bird Treaty Act. Photo: ©Marilyn Barnes

SPLAYS

Splays is a matched set of elbow-length arm warmers and scarf with channels of eyelets ending in pleats. The pleats on the arm warmers cover the back of the hand for warmth while leaving the palm exposed. The arm warmers start flat with the pleats and then the work is joined in the round and the sleeves are knit. The scarf uses lifted increases to create pleats at the end that visually match the pleats at the start.

SIZES
One Size

FINISHED MEASUREMENTS
Scarf: 60 inches / 152.5 cm long X 5.5 inches / 14 cm wide (unblocked)
Arm Warmers: 13 inches / 33 cm long (unstretched, including ruffle)

MATERIALS
Yarn: Knit Picks City Tweed DK (55% merino wool, 25% superfine alpaca, 20% donegal tweed; 123 yards/50 grams); color: Emerald Isle; scarf 365 yards, arm warmers 185 yards.

Needles: US #6 / 4 mm straight needles, or size needed to obtain gauge (for both)
Set of 5 US #6 / 4 mm double pointed needles, or size needed to obtain gauge (arm warmers only)

Tapestry needle

GAUGE
20 sts and 26 rows = 4 inches / 10 cm in stockinette stitch (unblocked)

PATTERN NOTES

I chose not to block the finished pieces to preserve the three dimensionality of the ribbing and the deep ruffles.

SPECIAL STITCHES AND TECHNIQUES

Cdd (central double decrease): Sl 2 sts together knitwise, k1, pass the 2 slipped stitches over the knit stitch.

Lifted double increase (LDI): Knit into the RH leg of the stitch below the next stitch on LH needle, knit into the back loop of stitch on the needle dropping the st off the LH needle, knit into the LH leg of the stitch below.

Lifted increase left (LIL): Knit the stitch on the needle as usual, then pick up the LH leg of the stitch below the one you just knit into with the LH needle and knit into it.

Lifted increase right (LIR): Knit into the RH leg of the stitch below the next stitch on LH needle, then knit into the stitch on the needle as usual.

PATTERN
Scarf

CO 86 sts.

Row 1 (WS): K2, *p5, k2; rep from * to end of row.

Row 2 (RS): K1, p1, k5, *p2, k5; rep from * to last 2 sts, p1, k1.

Rep rows 1 & 2 four more times (five reps total.)

Row 3: K2, *p5, k2; rep from * to end of row.

Row 4: K1, p1, ssk, k1, k2tog, *p2, ssk, k1, k2tog; rep from * to last 2 sts, p1, k1.

Row 5: K2, *p3, k2; rep from * to end of row.

Row 6: K1, p1, cdd, *p2, cdd; rep from * to last 2 sts, p1, k1.

Row 7: K2, *p1, k2; rep from * to end of row.

Row 8: K1, p1, k2, yo, ssk, *p2, k2, yo, ssk; rep from * to last 2 sts, p1, k1.

Row 9: K2 p2, yo, p2tog, *k2, p2, yo, p2tog; rep from * to last 2 sts, k2.

Rep rows 8 and 9 until the scarf is 58 inches / 147.25 cm or 2 inches / 5 cm shorter than the desired finished length.

Row 16: K1, p1, k2, yo, ssk, *p2, k2, yo, ssk; rep from * to last 2 sts, p1, k1.

Row 17: K2, *P1, K2; rep from * to last 3 sts, p1, k2.

Row 18: K1, p2, *LDI, p2; rep from * to last 3 sts, LDI, p1, k1.

Row 19: K2, *p3, k2; rep from * to end of row.

Row 20: K1, p1, *LIR, k1, LIL, p2; rep from * to last 5 sts, LIR, k1, LIL, p1, k1.

Row 21: K2, *p5, k2; rep from * to end of row.

Row 22: K1, p1, *k5, p2; rep from * to last 7 sts, k5, p1, k1.

Rep rows 21 & 22 four more times (five reps total).

Row 23: K2, *p5, k2; rep from * to end of row.

BO all sts.

Weave in loose ends.

Arm Warmers
Ruffle (knit flat)
CO 72 st.
Row 1 (WS): K2, *p5, k2; rep from * to end of row.
Row 2 (RS): K1, m1, p1, k5, *p2, k5; rep from * to last 2 sts, p1, m1, k1
Row 3: K3, p5, *k2, p5; rep from * to last 3 sts, k3.
Row 4: K1, m1, *p2, k5; rep from * to last 3 sts, p2, m1, k1.
Row 5: K1, p1, *k2, p5; rep from * to last 4 sts, k2, p1, k1.
Row 6: K1, m1, k1, *p2, k5; rep from * to last 4 sts, p2, k1, m1, k1.
Row 7: K1, p2, *k2, p5; rep from * to last 5 sts, k2, p2, k1.
Row 8: K3, *p2, k5; rep from * to last 5 sts, p2, k3.
Row 9: K1, p2, *k2, p5; rep from * to last 5 sts, k2, p2, k1.
Rep rows 8 & 9 one more time.

Row 10: K1, k2tog, p2, *ssk, k1, k2tog, p2; rep from * to last 3 sts, ssk, k1.
Row 11: K1, p1, *k2, p3; rep from * to last 4 sts, k2, p1, k1.
Row 12: K2, *p2, cdd; rep from * to last 4 sts, p2, k2. - 36 sts

Sleeve
Transfer the sts to the DPNs and join in the round, taking care not to twist the work.
Slip the first stitch on the first needle onto the last needle (first stitch becomes last stitch now.)
Rnd 1: *K1, p2; rep from * to end of rnd.
Rnd 2: *K2, yo, ssk, p2; rep from * to end of rnd.

Rnd 3: *K2tog, yo, k2, p2; rep from * to end of rnd.
Rep rnds 2 and 3 until the sleeve is 9 inches / 22.75 cm or 2 inches / 5 cm shorter than the desired finished length.

Cuff
Rnd 4: *K4, p2; rep from * to end of rnd.
Work rnd 4 until you have 2 inches / 5 cm of ribbing.
BO all sts using a stretchy bind off.
Weave in loose ends.

Barred Owl in the Bogue Chitto National Wildlife Refuge, Pearl River, Louisana; Photo: ©Robin Gill

MAINE COASTAL ISLANDS NATIONAL WILDLIFE REFUGE

The Maine Coastal Islands National Wildlife Refuge is a complex of smaller refuges that includes four coastal parcels and 61 islands. It spans more than 250 miles of coastline and protects over 8,200 acres of diverse habitat. Because of the wide variation from island to island, the refuge supports a dizzying diversity of wildlife. Stands of red spruce and balsam fir are used by nesting bald eagles and assorted wading birds, while areas of mixed grasses and raspberries support nesting terns, common eiders, and a number of neotropical migrants. Rocky ledges provide nest sites for Atlantic puffins, razorbills, black guillemots, and other seabirds. Rich intertidal zones and easy access to shoals of small fish offshore provide an abundance of food for the over 300 species of birds that use the refuge.

Conservation efforts within the refuge are focused on restoring nesting seabird populations. The small, isolated coastal islands once teemed with breeding colonies of gulls, terns, eiders, razorbills, cormorants, and puffins. But like so many of the birds mentioned in this book, their populations were decimated by the feather and egg trade. The great auk was extinct by the mid-1800s and many other species were on the brink. By the mid-1900s, conservationists began setting aside some of the breeding grounds used by the remaining birds. However, conservation alone wasn't enough. The larger, more aggressive gull species thrived around humans and took over the abandoned islands. With large colonies of predatory gulls established, the islands were no longer suitable breeding grounds for the smaller birds. Human intervention was needed to restore the breeding populations of terns, puffins, and other seabirds.

The charismatic Atlantic puffin with its plump little body and brightly colored bill is the perfect ambassador for seabird conservation. I first saw a picture of an Atlantic puffin when I was seven years old and I have been smitten ever since. In 1973, the National Audubon Society started Project Puffin with the hope of restoring puffins to their breeding grounds in Maine. The first attempt was made on Eastern Egg Rock, part of The Maine Coastal Islands National Wildlife Refuge, where a breeding population had flourished until 1885. After removing the predatory gulls from the island, researchers brought in puffin chicks from colonies in Canada. The chicks were placed in burrows on the island, and hand reared. The chicks fledged and headed out to sea but the researchers wouldn't really know if their efforts had been successful for several years. Then, in June of 1977, the first of the relocated chicks returned. Researchers used wooden decoys and recordings of puffin calls to lure the young birds to the island and to encourage them to explore nesting sites. The efforts worked and young birds were often seen sitting at the entrance to a burrow in the company of a decoy. By 1981, four breeding pairs were nesting on the island.

Today there are 150 pairs of puffins nesting on Eastern Egg Rock, and the program has been expanded to other islands. The same efforts that benefited the puffins have also helped terns, guillemots, petrels, and razor-bills. Seven of the islands in The Maine Coastal Islands National Wildlife Refuge now support seabird restoration projects. Researchers continue to closely monitor the seabird populations as global climate change again threatens the delicate balance. But for now the efforts of a dedicated group of researchers and volunteers have paid off and a wide array of seabirds, including the cunning little puffins, can once again be seen returning to their nests with beaks full of fish for their waiting chicks.

Atlantic Puffin at Maine Coastal Islands National Wildlife Refuge; Photo: U.S. Fish and Wildlife Service - Northeast Region

HERE BE PUFFINS

Where Maine's rocky shore meets the cold Atlantic Ocean is the land of puffins. Here Be Puffins is a crescent-shaped shawl that starts with a large section of stockinette stitch and gradually gives way to an undulating fan lace pattern. Pick a semi-solid and a coordinating variegated for a subtle look or two different solids for a stronger contrast.

SIZES
One size

FINISHED MEASUREMENTS
Length 66 inches / 167.5 cm
Width 15 inches / 38 cm

MATERIALS
Yarn: Knit Picks Hawthorne Fingering (80% superwash fine highland wool, 20% polyamide; 357 yards/100 grams); colors: Conifer Kettle Dye (land), Vancouver (sea); 1 skein each

Needles: 40 inch US#6 / 4mm circular needle, or size needed to obtain gauge

Stitch marker
Tapestry needle

GAUGE
20 sts and 32 rows = 4 inches / 10 cm in stockinette stitch

Pattern Notes

As written this pattern will use the entire skein of sea colored yarn. If your gauge is looser than specified you will need to use a second skein or finish the piece using the land colored yarn.

Special Stitches and Techniques

Kyok (knit, yarn over, knit): Knit, then yo, then knit again into the the same st. Three sts made from 1 st.

Pattern

Set-Up

With "land" colored yarn, CO 8 sts placing a marker in the center.

Row 1 (WS): K2, yo, k4, yo, k2.

Row 2 (RS): K2, kyok, knit to last 3 sts, kyok, k2.

Row 3: K2, yo, purl to last 2 sts, yo, k2.

Rep rows 2 and 3 until you have 172 sts.

Row 4: K2, kyok, knit to last 3 sts, kyok, k2. 176 sts.

Row 5: K2, purl to last 2 sts, yo, k2. (Note that you DO NOT make a yo after the k2 at the beginning of this row.)

Leave yarn attached and push the sts to the opposite end of the circular needle so you are set up to work another WS row.

Switch to "sea" colored yarn.

Row 6 (WS): K2, yo, knit to marker, remove marker and turn the work.

Row 7 (RS): Sl1, k2, [(k1, yo) x10, k1, p1] six times, (k1, yo) x10, k1, kyok, k2.

Skip to row 3 of body section below.

Body

Row 1 (WS): K2, yo, knit all sea sts, m1, k2tog, k25, turn.

Row 2 (RS): Sl1, k2, [(k1, yo) x10, k1, p1] ten times, (k1, yo) x10, k1, kyok, k2.

Row 3: K2, yo, knit all sea sts, m1, k3, turn.

Row 4: Sl1, k1, ssk, k3, [ssk, k17, k2tog, p1] six times, ssk, k17, k2tog, k3, kyok, k2.
Row 5: K2, yo, p6, [p2tog, p15, p2togb, k1] six times, p2tog, p15, p2togb, p6, m1, k3, turn.
Row 6: Sl1, k1, ssk, k6, [ssk, k13, k2tog, p1] six times, ssk, k13, k2tog, k6, kyok, k2.
Row 7: K2, yo, p9, [p2tog, p11, p2togb, k1] six times, p2tog, p11, p2togb, p9, m1, k3, turn.
Row 8: Sl1, k1, ssk, k9, [ssk, k9, k2tog, p1] six times, ssk, k9, k2tog, k9, kyok, k2.
Row 9: K2, yo, knit all sea sts, m1, k3, turn.
Row 10: Sl1, k1, ssk, [(k1, yo) x10, k1, p1] eight times, (k1, yo) x10, k1, kyok, k2.
Rep rows 3 - 8 once working four additional reps of the bracketed section in each row.
Leave yarn attached and push the sts to the opposite end of the circular needle so you are set up to work another RS row.

Switch to "land" colored yarn.
Row 11 (RS): K2, kyok, knit all land sts, m1, k3.
Row 12 (WS): Sl1, p1, p2tog, purl to last 2 sts, yo, k2.
Rep rows 11 and 12 seven more times (eight reps total.)
Leave yarn attached and push the sts to the opposite end of the circular needle so you are set up to work another WS row.

Rep body section (starting with row 1) three more times (four reps total.) Each time you work the sea colored yarn add 4 more reps to the bracketed sections.
Cut the land colored yarn after last rep.

Edge and Bind Off
Row 1 (WS): K2, yo, knit to last sea st, k2tog, knit to last 5 sts, ssk, yo, ssk, k1.
Row 2 (RS): K2, kyok, [(k1, yo) x10, k1, p1] twenty-nine times, (k1, yo) x10, k1, kyok, k2.
Row 3: K2, yo, knit to last 2 sts, yo, k2.
Work this last row binding off each st after you work it.
Row 4: K6, [ssk, k17, k2tog, p1] twenty-nine times, ssk, k17, k2tog, k6.

Weave in loose ends.
Block taking care to create the scalloped edge and crescent shape.

EVERGLADES NATIONAL PARK

The Florida Everglades is a complex system of wetlands that once extended from Orlando to the southern tip of the Florida peninsula. Water flowed unimpeded from the Kissimmee River to Lake Okeechobee and on south, spilling over low-lying land to coastal estuaries. There was a shallow, slow moving sheet of water that covered over five million acres, feeding a patchwork of ponds, sloughs, sawgrass marshes, hardwood hammocks, and forest uplands.

In the late 1800s people began draining land for development and agriculture. By the 1920s drainage efforts had been effective enough to create a land boom in south Florida. Towns and cities sprang up, displacing native plants and animals. People built more canals and levees to protect these new communities from flooding, which further impeded water flow to the wetlands. However, flooding continued until the construction of a four story wall, called the Herbert Hoover Dike, around Lake Okeechobee effectively cut off the water supply to the Everglades.

Everglades National Park was established in 1947 to protect the remaining South Florida wetlands from development, making it the largest sub-tropical wilderness in the US and the first park created to protect a specific ecosystem. Although the land was now protected as a national park, flood control measures north of the park continued to starve the Everglades of vital water. In the 1960s, the Army Corps of Engineers, responsible for administering the flood control measures, was directed to provide the park with sufficient water but did not follow through on the mandate. In 1972, environmental groups successfully lobbied to pass a bill that curbed development in South Florida and ensured that the park got the water it needed.

Today Everglades National Park encompasses 1.5 million acres of wetlands. It is the most significant breeding ground for wading birds in North America and is home to 36 endangered species including the Florida panther, American crocodile, and the West Indian manatee. But the fight is not over. If these and so many more species are to survive, we must continue to push to ensure that the Everglades, and the water that is its lifeblood, are protected.

Everglades National Park protects the largest contiguous stand of mangrove trees in the northern hemisphere. The mangroves possess a complex root system that enables them to thrive in the brackish water of the inter-tidal zone. Those prominent, twining roots, called prop roots, provide nesting sites, cover, and foraging grounds for a wide assortment of marine invertebrates as well as fish, birds, reptiles, and small mammals. The dense stands of mangrove also buffer the effects of storms by acting as a wind break and by baffling wave action. The tangle of interlaced prop roots helps stabilize the shoreline, reducing erosion and enhancing water clarity. The mangrove roots filter runoff, trapping sediment and debris, further improving water quality. The mangrove forests are a vital part of the estuarine and marine environments as well as being one of the most recognizable symbols of the Florida Everglades.

Mangrove Island; Photo: David Grimes, Everglades National Park Service

MANGROVE

Mangrove is a pair of fingerless mitts adorned with an all-over lacy pattern of intertwining stitches. They have a slightly flared cuff and a gusset thumb. While the pattern looks intricate, it's pretty straightforward and fun to knit.

SIZES
One Size

FINISHED MEASUREMENTS
Hand circumference 6 inches / 15.25 cm (unstretched)

MATERIALS
Yarn: Knit Picks Hawthorne Fingering (80% superwash wool, 20% polyamide; 357 yards/100 grams); color: Serpent Kettle Dye; 1 skein

Needles: Set of 4 US #1 / 2.25 mm double pointed needles, or size needed to obtain gauge

Stitch marker
Stitch holder or scrap yarn
Tapestry needle

GAUGE
34 sts and 48 rnds = 4 inches /10 cm in stockinette stitch

SPECIAL STITCHES AND TECHNIQUES

Cdd (central double decrease): Sl 2 sts together knitwise, k1, pass the 2 slipped stitches over the knit stitch.

Stretchy bind off: K2, place tip of LH needle into fronts of these 2 sts, k2tog, *k1, place tip of LH needle into fronts of these 2 sts, k2tog, rep from * until all sts have been bound off.

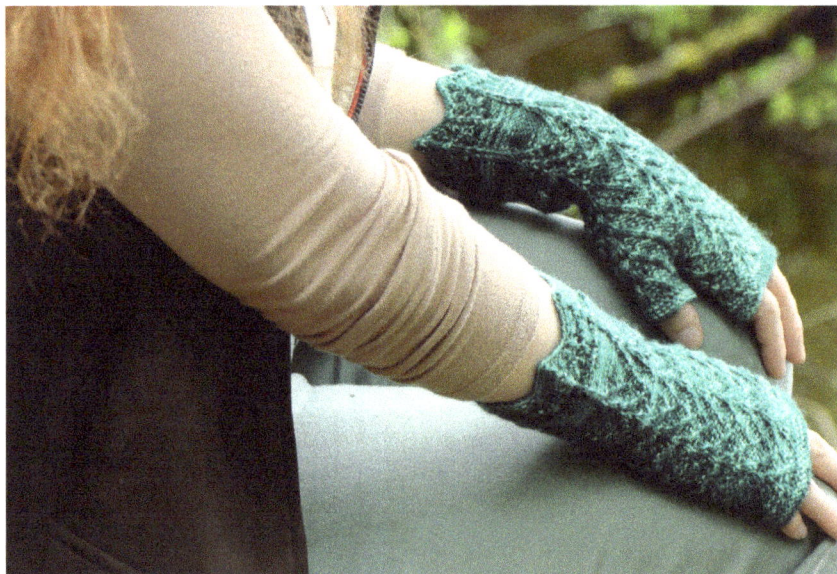

PATTERN

Cuff

CO 72 sts distributed evenly across 3 needles and join in the round taking care not to twist the work.

Rnd 1: Purl.

Rnd 2: *K1, yo, k4, cdd, k4, yo; rep from * to end of rnd.

Rnd 3: Knit.

Rnd 4: *K1, yo, ssk, yo, ssk, yo, cdd, yo, k2tog, yo, k2tog, yo; rep from * to end of rnd.

Rnd 5: Knit.

Rnd 6: *K1, yo, k4, cdd, k4, yo; rep from * to end of rnd.

Rep rnds 1 - 6 one more time.

Rnd 7: *P6, k1, p5; rep from * to end of rnd.

Rep rnd 7 seven more times.

Work Chart 1 once (6 reps per rnd.) - 54 sts

Thumb Gusset

Work 5 reps of Chart 2 over the first 45 sts and 1 rep of Chart 3 over the last 9 sts of the rnd.

(Please note that Charts 2 and 3 are placed in reverse order to match the direction of knitting.)

Continue in this pattern until all rnds of Charts 2 and 3 have been worked once.

Next Rnd: [P2, k1, p1, k1, p3, k1] five times, p2, place the next 17 st onto scrap yarn, CO 5, p2.

CHART 1

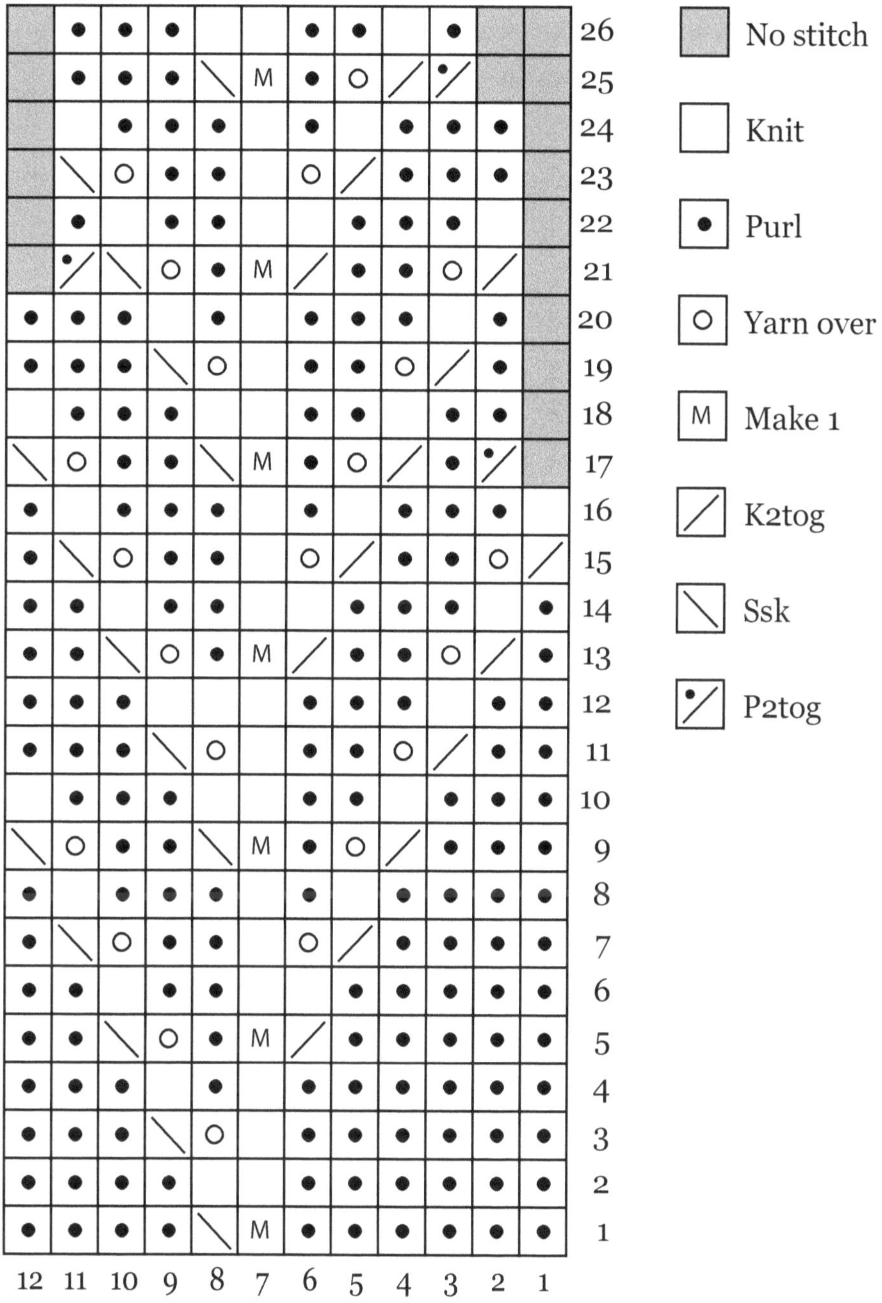
No stitch
Knit
Purl
Yarn over
Make 1
K2tog
Ssk
P2tog

CHART 3

21	20	19	18	17	16	15	14	13	12	11	10	9	8	7	6	5	4	3	2	1	
•	•	\	○	•	•	\	○	•	•		○	/	•	•	○	/	•	•	•	•	29
•	•	•		•	•	•		•	•		•	•	•		•	•	•			•	28
•	•	•	\	○	•	•	\	○	•	M	/	•	•	○	/	•	•	•	○	/	27
M	•	•	•		•	•	•		•		•	•	•		•	•	•		•	M	26
	•	•	•	\	○	•	•	\	○		•	•	○	/	•	•	•	○	/	•	25
	•	•	•	•		•	•	•		•	•	•		•	•	•		•	•		24
	•	•	•	•	\	○	•	•	\	M	•	○	/	•	•	○	/	•	•		23
	•		•	•	•		•	•	•		•		•	•	•		•	•	•		22
	M	\	○	•	•	\	○	•	•		○	/	•	•	○	/	•	•	M		21
		•		•	•	•		•	•		•	•	•		•	•	•				20
		•	\	○	•	•	\	○	•	M	/	•	•	○	/	•	•	•			19
		•	•		•	•	•		•		•	•	•		•	•	•				18
		•	•	\	○	•	•	\	○		•	•	○	/	•	•	•				17
		M	•	•		•	•	•		•	•		•	•	•		M				16
			•	•	\	○	•	•	\	M	•	○	/	•	•	○	/				15
			•	•	•		•	•	•		•	•	•		•						14
			•	•	•	\	○	•	•		○	/	•	•	○	/	•				13
			•	•	•	•		•	•		•	•	•		•	•					12
			M	•	•	•	\	○	•	M	/	•	•	○	/	•	M				11
				•	•	•		•	•		•	•	•		•	•					10
				\	○	•	•	\	○		•	•	○	/	•	•					9
				•		•	•	•		•	•		•	•	•						8
				•	\	○	•	•	\	M	•	○	/	•	•	•					7
				M	•		•	•	•		•		•	•	•	M					6
				•	•	\	○	•	•		○	/	•	•	•						5
				•	•		•	•	•		•	•	•								4
				•	•	\	○	•	M	/	•	•	○	/							3
				•	•	•		•	•		•	•	•	•							2
				M	•	•	\	○	•	•	○	/	M								1

CHART 2

9	8	7	6	5	4	3	2	1	
\	O	•	•		O	/	•	•	29
•		•	•			•	•	•	28
•	\	O	•	M	/	•	•	•	27
•	•		•		•	•	•		26
•	•	\	O		•	•	O	/	25
•	•	•			•	•		•	24
•	•	•	\	M	•	O	/	•	23
	•	•	•		•		•	•	22
\	O	•	•		O	/	•	•	21
•		•	•			•	•	•	20
•	\	O	•	M	/	•	•	•	19
•	•		•		•	•	•		18
•	•	\	O		•	•	O	/	17
•	•	•			•	•		•	16
•	•	•	\	M	•	O	/	•	15
	•	•	•		•		•	•	14
\	O	•	•		O	/	•	•	13
•		•	•			•	•	•	12
•	\	O	•	M	/	•	•	•	11
•	•		•		•	•	•		10
•	•	\	O		•	•	O	/	9
•	•	•			•	•		•	8
•	•	•	\	M	•	O	/	•	7
	•	•	•		•		•	•	6
\	O	•	•		O	/	•	•	5
•		•	•			•	•	•	4
•	\	O	•	M	/	•	•	•	3
•	•		•		•	•	•		2
•	•	\	O		•	•	O	/	1

Rnd 31: Purl.
Rep rnds 30 and 31 two more times (three reps total.)
BO all sts using the stretchy bind off.

Thumb
Place the 17 sts from the scrap yarn back onto the needles, pick up 5 sts knitwise at the hand, pm to mark end of rnd.
Work all rnds of Chart 4 once over the first 17 sts, knitting the remaining 5 sts of each rnd.
Rnd 11: Knit.
Rnd 12: Purl.
Rep rnds 11 and 12 two more times (three reps total.)
BO all sts using the stretchy bind off.

Weave in loose ends.
Block gently.

Repeat for second mitt.

Hand
Work rows 7 - 29 of Chart 2 once (6 reps per rnd.)
Rnd 30: Knit.

CHART 4

17	16	15	14	13	12	11	10	9	8	7	6	5	4	3	2	1	
•	•	•	\	O	•	•	•		•	O	/	•	•	O	/	•	10
	•	•	•		•	•	•		•		•	•	•		•	•	9
\	O	•	•	\	O	•	•		O	/	•	•	O	/	•	•	8
•		•	•	•		•	•		•	•	•		•	•	•	•	7
•	\	O	•	•	\	O	•	M	/	•	•	O	/	•	•	•	6
•	•		•	•	•		•		•	•	•		•	•	•		5
•	•	\	O	•	•	\	O		•	•	O	/	•	•	O	/	4
•	•	•		•	•	•			•	•		•	•	•		•	3
•	•	•	\	O	•	•	\	M	•	O	/	•	•	O	/	•	2
	•	•	•		•	•	•		•		•	•	•		•	•	1

"I was delighted to stumble upon this wetland after a long hike to Tensleep Lake in the Bighorn Mountains. In a cool landscape dominated by deep green spruce and light grey granite boulders, the lively green of the wetland plants was such a bright surprise."

Bighorn National Forest Near Tensleep Lake, Wyoming
Photo: ©Elizabeth Fisher

ONE OF MY FAVORITE PLACES ON EARTH AND AN ENCOUNTER WITH AN AWFUL LOT OF GEESE

In addition to its vital importance to migratory birds, and its iconic status with birders all around the world, Malheur National Wildlife Refuge has great sentimental meaning for me. My graduate school thesis advisor, Professor Richard Forbes, was an avid birder. Every spring he would gather up his ornithology class and any grad students who wanted to tag along and take us to the southeastern corner of Oregon where the refuge is located. We'd spend a dizzying, jam-packed four days crisscrossing the region, investigating anything and everything we could find; pronghorn, badgers, marmots, assorted small rodents, lizards and snakes (including the baby rattlesnake Prof. Forbes insisted on picking up), and birds, oh the birds! It wasn't just the animals; the land itself held lessons in ecology and geology. At night, in that remote darkness, the sky bloomed with stars. I've visited a number of times since those grad school trips and always find something new to marvel at, something I hadn't noticed before. It is a place that fills my soul with reckless glee. It is a place of awe and wonder and quiet memories of times and people now past.

I was back at the refuge some years later with a couple of friends, for a spring birding trip. We had stopped at the side of the road to scan a pond hoping to find wading birds along the muddy edges. As I stood there I gradually became aware of what I can only describe as a thrumming. I felt it before I actually heard it; the air was alive. We searched the horizon, trying the locate the source as the intensity of the sound increased. And then, there it was, the largest flock of geese I'd ever seen. I stood slack-jawed as the mass of snow geese came toward us. We were cast into shadow as the living canopy passed overhead. Their honking mixed with the sound of air running through their feathers with each wingbeat created a cacophony so intense that my own body vibrated with it. I had no choice but to laugh with pure, wild joy! The geese flew on, indifferent to the reactions of the people standing below, and I was left breathless, with yet another reminder of the awesome power and beauty of the natural world.

Malheur Wildlife Refuge

Malheur National Wildlife Refuge

With its three large lakes (Malheur, Mud, and Harney), Malheur National Wildlife Refuge provides a much needed oasis in the high desert of Oregon. The refuge was established by President Roosevelt to protect birds such as the snowy egret, prized for its plumes, from being hunted to extinction for the feather trade. Located on the Pacific Flyway, Malheur plays host to an enormous array of birds throughout the year. Some are just stopping by mid-migration for a quick rest and are on their way again. Others use the lush habitats found on the refuge as a summer breeding ground. And yet others live there year round. In a typical year, more than 320 bird species will spend time on the refuge.

In 2016 the Malheur Wildlife Refuge headquarters was occupied by a group of heavily armed, anti-government militants who considered the ownership of land by the federal government to be governmental overreach. They objected to the designation of federal land (such as national parks and refuges) set aside for conservation and enjoyment of all. Instead they felt those lands should be administered locally to the benefit of the local residents, and in their case that meant cattle grazing. The standoff lasted six weeks and left one militant dead and another 26 under arrest. The occupiers caused significant damage to the headquarters buildings and surrounding land. They damaged Native American artifacts and desecrated sacred sites. The occupation interrupted conservation and research projects on the refuge. The disruption set back an effort to reduce the population of invasive carp in Malheur Lake by at least three years.

Federally controlled wildlife refuges like Malheur play a key role in protecting endangered species, such as the greater sage-grouse. One of the more flamboyant year round residents of the refuge, the greater sage-grouse inhabits sagebrush grasslands on the refuge and throughout the western United States. Each spring the males gather on breeding grounds called leks, where each one stakes out a small area and begins an elaborate "strutting display." They are hoping to attract the attention of the females who come to pick their perfect mate. Sage-grouse populations have declined due to habitat loss, and the federally protected land where they live is a vital part of ensuring that the sage-grouse will continue to strut for generations to come.

Museum Building at Malheur Wildlife Refuge Headquarters at Dusk

SAGE-GROUSE

Sage-Grouse is an easy to knit asymmetrical garter stitch shawlette. The unusual design features fan motifs that dance along the top edge of the piece. They are knit one at a time between sections of garter stitch, which breaks up the work and keeps the knitting interesting. The shawlette gets bigger as it goes allowing the knitter to easily customize the size as desired.

SIZES
One Size (Size is adjustable depending on amount of yarn used. Sample shown uses the entire skein of yarn.)

FINISHED MEASUREMENTS
45 inches / 114.25cm long

MATERIALS
Yarn: Knit Picks Hawthorne Fingering (80% superwash wool, 20% polyamide; 357 yards/100 grams); color: City Lights Speckle; 1 skein

Needles: Two 24 inch US #5 / 3.75 mm circular needles, or size needed to obtain gauge

GAUGE
20 sts and 40 rows = 4 inches / 10 cm in garter stitch

SPECIAL STITCHES AND TECHNIQUES

Central Double Increase: K1 through the back loop and the front loop of one stitch, then insert LH needle point behind the vertical strand that runs between the 2 sts just made, and k1 through back loop of this strand to make 3rd stitch of group

CHART 1

21	20	19	18	17	16	15	14	13	12	11	10	9	8	7	6	5	4	3	2	1	
V		•	•		•	•		•	•		•	•		•	•		•	•		•	**16**
	M	•	\	M	•	\	M	•	•	M	/	•	M	/	•	M			V		15
	V		•	•		•			•	•			•	•			•				**14**
		M	•	\	M	•	\	M		M	/	•	M	/	•	M		V			13
		V		•	•		•	•			•	•		•	•		•				**12**
			M	•	\	M	•/	M		M	•/	M	/	•	M		V				11
			V		•	•		•	•		•	•		•	•		•				**10**
				M	•	\	M	•		•	M	/	•	M		V					9
					M	•	\	M		M	/	•	M		V						**8**
						M	•	\	M		M	/	•	M		V					7
						V		•	•			•	•		•						**6**
							M	•/	M		M	•/	M		V						5
							V		•	•		•	•		•						**4**
								M	•		•	M		V							3
								V		•		•		•							**2**
									⋁			V									1

PATTERN

Set-Up
With the first needle, CO 5 sts.
Knit 1 row.
Work Chart 1 once.
BO 10 sts purlwise, p10.
With the second needle and working from the RS, pick up knitwise 14 sts along the left selvedge.
Knit 5 rows.

Body
Working from the WS, with the RH tip of the first needle pick up knitwise 4 sts along the selvedge of the section just knit. You will also have 11 sts on the LH tip of the needle from the previous section. Turn the work.
Work Chart 2 once.
BO 9 sts purlwise, p10.
With the second needle and working from the RS, pick up

CHART 2

Row	20	19	18	17	16	15	14	13	12	11	10	9	8	7	6	5	4	3	2	1	Row
16	V		•	•		•	•		•	•		•	•		•	•		•	•	/	
		M	•	\	M	•	\	M	•		•	M	/	•	M	/	•	M	V		15
14	▓	V		•	•		•	•		•		•		•	•		•	•	/	▓	
	▓		M	•	\	M	•	\	M	M	/	•	M	/	•	M	V	▓			13
12	▓		V		•	•		•	•		•	•		•	•	/3	▓				
	▓			M	•	\	M	•/	M	M	•/	M	/	•	M	V	▓				11
10	▓			V		•	•		•	•		•	•		•	/	▓	▓			
	▓	▓			M	•	\	M	•		•	M	/	•	M	V	▓	▓			9
8	▓	▓		V		•	•		•		•	•	/3	▓	▓	▓					
	▓	▓	▓		M	•	\	M	M	/	•	M	V	▓	▓	▓					7
6	▓	▓	▓	V		•	•			•	•	/	▓	▓	▓	▓					
	▓	▓	▓	▓	M	•/	M	M	•/	M	V	▓	▓	▓	▓	▓					5
4	▓	▓	▓	▓	V		•	•		•	•	/3	▓	▓	▓	▓					
	▓	▓	▓	▓	▓	M	•		•	M	V	▓	▓	▓	▓	▓					3
2	▓	▓	▓	▓	▓	▓	V		•		•	/	▓	▓	▓	▓					
	▓	▓	▓	▓	▓	▓	▓	▓	▓	▓	W		V	▓	▓	▓					1

Legend

- ▓ No stitch
- (blank) Knit
- • Purl
- V Slip
- M Make 1
- W Central Double Inc
- / K2tog
- \ Ssk
- /3 K3tog
- •/ P2tog

knitwise 14 sts along the left selvedge.
Knit the remaining sts on the second needle.
Knit 5 rows.

Rep the body section until you've used almost all the yarn (or the shawl is the desired length) ending after the 4th knit row.

End
BO all sts on the second needle.
Pick up 4 sts as before and work
Chart 2 once.
BO all sts purlwise.

FINISHING:
Block flat taking care to shape the
fans and create the curve of the
shawlette. Remember that the lace
pattern is at the top of this piece.

Fort Rock in the Oregon Outback; Photo: ©Jan Just

Necedah National Wildlife Refuge

The Necedah National Wildlife Refuge, located in central Wisconsin, was established in 1939 and protects over 43,000 acres of "the Great Wisconsin Swamp." This mosaic of habitats includes sedge meadow, savanna, prairie, and pine-oak forest. One of the primary missions of the refuge is to provide habitat for threatened and rare species. Over the years this commitment to wildlife restoration has seen the successful reintroduction of Canada geese in 1939, wild turkeys in 1952, mallards in the 1960s, and trumpeter swans in 1994. Recently, the refuge has added the propagation of milkweed plants, the main food for monarch butterfly caterpillars, to its list of restoration projects.

Today, less than 10,000 acres of savanna remain of Wisconsin's original 4.1 million acres. Savanna restoration projects in the Necedah National Wildlife Refuge were started in 1959. Through careful plant propagation the refuge staff have successfully created over 3000 acres of savanna and brought back species lost from the area since the 1930s. The restored savanna is now home to more than 110 species of migratory birds, three species of amphibians, 14 species of reptiles, and 44 species of butterflies, including the monarch butterfly.

The brightly colored, orange and black monarch butterfly is probably the most easily recognized species of butterfly in North America. It is found throughout the US and is an important pollinator of food crops and other plants. In the last couple of decades researchers have measured a significant decline in overwintering populations, sparking concern. While the monarch is not yet federally protected, it was designated a species of concern for the Pollinator Health Task Force created in 2014 by President Obama.

There are a number of probable factors for the butterfly's decline, including the use of pesticides, climate change, and habitat loss. These are threats to bees and other pollinators as well as monarchs and must be addressed in order to save the pollinators that play a key role in so much of our food production.

Unlike other pollinators, monarchs are completely dependent on only one type of plant, milkweed, for their reproduction. The females lay their eggs on milkweeds, where the larvae hatch and feed exclusively on their leaves. The milkweed plants produce a toxin that the monarchs are able to ingest and store in their bodies rendering them poisonous to most predators.

One of the most straightforward things we can do to help monarch butterflies is to plant milkweed. There are a variety of species to choose from that will grow in a wide range of climates. The plants make a nice addition to a garden and you will reap the benefits of attracting butterflies and other pollinators to your yard.

Monarch Butterfly; Photo: ©Marilyn Barnes

MILKWEED AND MONARCHS

Milkweed seeds and butterfly motifs float across the fabric of this matched mitts and hat set. Using unusual but easy to learn techniques for creating the motifs, this pattern is perfect for the adventurous knitter.

SIZES
One size

FINISHED MEASUREMENTS
Hat: Band circumference 16 inch / 40.5 cm (unstretched)
Mitts: Hand circumference 7 inch / 17.75 cm (unstretched)

MATERIALS
Yarn: Knit Picks Swish DK (100% superwash merino wool; 123 yards/50 grams); color: Allspice; hat 155 yards, mitts 135 yards

Needles: Set of 5 US #3 / 3.25 mm double pointed needles
Set of 5 US #5 / 3.75 mm double pointed needles, or size needed to obtain gauge

Stitch holder or scrap yarn
Tapestry needle

GAUGE
20 sts and 28 rnds = 4 inches / 10 cm in stockinette stitch, with larger needles

PATTERN NOTES

The pattern is written assuming you will use a set of 5 double pointed needles with the stitches evenly distributed on the 4 needles. If you prefer to use the magic loop method on a circular needle, you will need to use stitch markers to mark the breaks between needles.

SPECIAL STITCHES AND TECHNIQUES

Rt (right twist): Knit into the second st on the LH needle without dropping the st off the needle, knit into the first st on the LH needle and drop both sts off the needle.

B (bundle): Place the tip of the RH needle under the 4 floating strands and into the st 3 rnds below the next st on the LH needle, pull up a loop and place it in the LH needle, ssk.

Stretchy bind off: K2, place tip of LH needle into fronts of these 2 sts, k2tog, *k1, place tip of LH needle into fronts of these 2 sts, k2tog, rep from * until all sts have been bound off.

Stitch Patterns
Baby Cable Rib
Rnd 1: *K2, p2, rt, p2; rep from * to end of rnd.
Rnd 2: *K2, p2; rep from * to end of rnd.
Rep Rnds 1 and 2 for pattern.

Pattern
Hat
With smaller needles, CO 120 sts evenly across 4 dpns. Join in the round, taking care not to twist the work.
Work 2 inches / 5 cm in baby cable rib.

Switch to larger needles.
Rnds 1 and 2: Knit.
Rnd 3: *Wyif sl7, k3; rep from * to end of rnd.
Rnd 4: Knit.
Rep Rnds 3 and 4 three more times (4 reps total.)
Rnd 5: *K3, b, k6; rep from * to end of rnd.
Slip the first 2 sts of the rnd so that they become the last 2 sts of the previous rnd and reposition sts as needed so there are 30 sts on each needle.
Rnds 6 - 10: Knit.

Rnd 11: *K4, locate the st 5 rnds below the 3rd st from the tip of the LH needle, insert the RH needle into this st and pull up a loop, k5, pull up another loop from the same st below, k1; rep from * to end of rnd.
Rnd 12: *K3, k2tog, k2, pull up a loop from the same st as before, k3, ssk; rep from * to end of rnd.

Rnd 13: *K6, ssk, k3; rep from * to end of rnd.
Sl the last 2 sts of the rnd back to the beginning of the rnd and reposition sts as needed so there are 30 sts on each needle.
Rnd 14: Sl2, knit to end of rnd.
Rnd 15: Knit.
Rnd 16: *Wyif sl7, k2tog, k1, [wyif sl7, k3] twice; rep from * to end of rnd. - 4 sts decreased
Rnd 17: Knit.
Rnd 18: *Wyif sl7, k2, [wyif sl7, k3] twice; rep from * to end of rnd.
Rnd 19: Knit.
Rnd 20: *Wyif sl7, k2, wyif sl7, k2tog, k1, wyif sl7, k3; rep from * to end of rnd. - 4 sts decreased
Rnd 21: Knit.
Rnd 22: *[Wyif sl7, k2] twice, wyif sl7, k3; rep from * to end of rnd.
Rnd 23: Knit.
Rnd 24: *K3, b, [k8, b] twice, k3, k2tog, k1; rep from * to end of rnd. - 4 sts decreased
Slip the first 3 sts of the rnd so that they becomes the last 3 sts of the previous rnd and reposition sts as needed so there are 27 sts on each needle.
Rnd 25: *K4, k2tog, k21; rep from * to end of rnd. - 4 sts decreased
Rnd 26: Knit
Rnd 27: *K12, k2tog, k12; rep from * to end of rnd. - 4 sts decreased
Rnd 28: Knit.
Rnd 29: *K20, k2tog, k3; rep from * to end of rnd. - 4 sts decreased
Rnd 30: *K2, locate the st 5 rnds below the 3rd st from the tip of the LH needle, insert the RH needle into this st and pull up a loop, k5, pull

up another loop from the same st below, k1; rep from * to end of rnd.
Rnd 32: *K1, k2tog, k2, pull up a loop from the same st as before, k3, ssk; rep from * to end of rnd.
Rnd 33: *K2tog, k2, ssk, k3; rep from * to end of rnd. - 12 sts decreased
Rnd 34: Knit.
Decr Rnds 35, 37, 39, 41, 45: *Ssk, knit to last 2 sts on the needle, k2tog; rep from * to end of rnd. - 8

sts decreased in each rnd
Rnd 36: *K6, wyif sl7, k6; rep from * to end of rnd.
Rnd 38: *K5, wyif sl7, k5; rep from * to end of rnd.
Rnd 40: *K4, wyif sl7, k4; rep from * to end of rnd.
Rnd 42: *K3, wyif sl7, k3; rep from * to end of rnd.
Rnd 43: *Ssk, k4, b, k4, k2tog; rep from * to end of rnd. - 8 sts decreased
Rnd 44: Knit.
Continue to alternate decr rnds and knit rnds until there are only 3 sts left on each needle.

Cut the yarn leaving a tail.
With a tapestry needle, thread the tail through the remaining sts and cinch tight to close the top.

Weave in loose ends.
Block gently to shape.

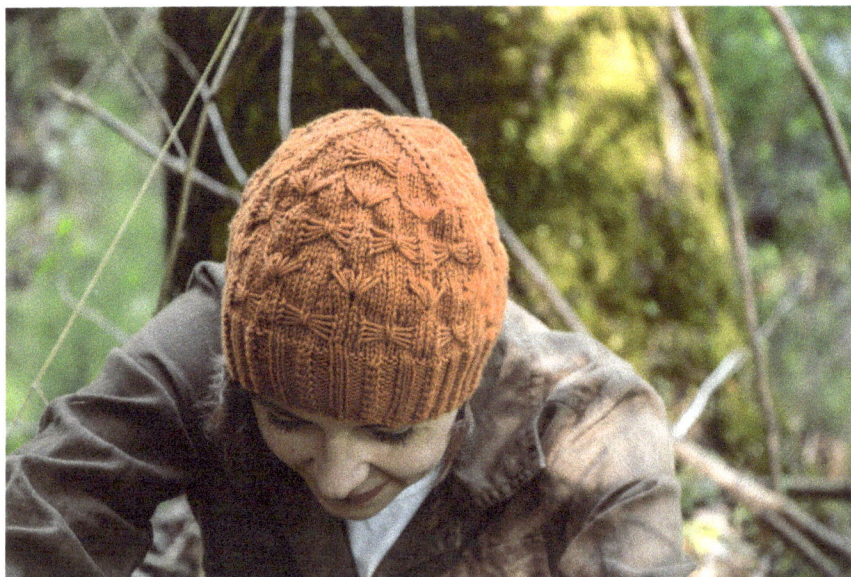

Mitts
Cuff
With larger needles, CO 40 sts evenly across 4 DPNs. Join sts to in the round, taking care not to twist the work. Place a stitch marker to denote the beginning of the rnd.
Rnd 1: Knit.
Rnd 2: Purl.
Rnd 3: Knit.
Rnd 4: Purl.
Rnd 5: Knit.

Rnd 6: *Wyif sl7, k3; rep from * to end of rnd.
Rnd 7: Knit.
Rep rnds 6 and 7 three more times (4 reps total.)
Rnd 8: *K3, b, k6; rep from * to end of rnd.
Slip the first 2 sts of the rnd so that they become the last 2 sts of the previous rnd and reposition sts as needed so there are 10 sts on each needle.
Rnds 9 - 13: Knit.
Rnd 14: *K4, locate the st 5 rnds below the 3rd st from the tip of the LH needle, insert the RH needle into this st and pull up a loop, k5, pull up another loop from the same st below, k1; rep from * to end of rnd.
Rnd 15: *K3, k2tog, k2, pull up a loop from the same st as before, k3, ssk; rep from * to end of rnd.
Rnd 16: *K6, ssk, k3; rep from * to end of rnd.
Sl the last 2 sts of the rnd back to the beginning of the rnd and reposition sts as needed so there are 10 sts on each needle.

Rnd 17: Sl2, knit to end of rnd.
Rnd 18: Knit.
Rep rnds 6 - 8.

Gusset
Rnd 19: Knit.
Rnd 20: K7, m1, k3, m1, knit to end of rnd.
Rnd 21 and 22: Knit.
Rnd 23: K7, m1, k5, m1, knit to end of rnd.

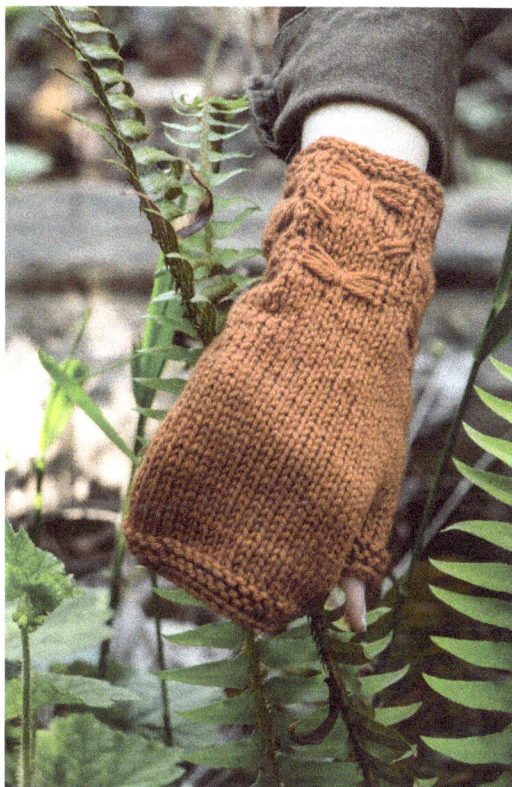

Rnd 24: K8, locate the st 5 rnds below the 3rd st from the tip of the LH needle, insert the RH needle into this st and pull up a loop, k5, pull up another loop from the same st below, knit to end of rnd.

Rnd 25: K7, k2tog, k2, pull up a loop from the same st as before, k3, ssk, knit to end of rnd.
Rnd 26: K7, m1, k3, ssk, k3, m1, knit to end of rnd.
Knit 8 rnds. (Add more rnds here if a taller gusset is needed.)

Hand
Rnd 27: K6, using the backward loop CO 2 sts, place the next 11 sts on scrap yarn, knit to end of rnd.
Work in stockinette st until the hand is 2.5 inches / 6.5 cm tall (or 0.5 inch / 1.25 cm shorter than desired hand height.)
Rnd 28: Purl.
Rnd 29: Knit.
Rnd 30: Purl.
Rnd 31: Knit.
BO all sts using the stretchy bind off.

Thumb
Place 11 sts from the scrap yarn onto needles. Pick up 2 sts from the CO edge at the hand.
Rnds 1 - 6: Knit
Rnd 7: Purl.
Rnd 8: Knit.
Rep rnds 7 and 8 one more time (2 reps total.)
BO all sts using the stretchy bind off.

Weave in loose ends.
Block gently.

Repeat for the second mitt.

Family of Canada Geese in the Reed College Canyon
Photo: ©Marilyn Barnes

GREAT SMOKY MOUNTAINS NATIONAL PARK

Protecting 187,000 acres of old growth forest, Great Smoky Mountains National Park was created in 1934 in response to the high rate of clearcutting in the area. The park now protects some of the most diverse ecosystems in North America, with 1600 species of flowering plants providing habitat for hundreds of species of mammals, birds, fish, amphibians, reptiles, and insects. Each year over 11 million people visit the park to enjoy its natural beauty and to learn about the biodiversity it protects, making it the most frequently visited of the national parks.

The Great Smoky Mountains National Park is home to nineteen species of fireflies. These bioluminescent beetles use flashes of light to attract mates. Each species has its own flash pattern, but synchronous fireflies are unique in that the males coordinate their displays. For a very brief period each spring, visitors are treated to a spectacular light show as large groups of male synchronous fireflies flash in unison, creating waves of light that wash across the hillsides.

While the fragile ecosystems of Great Smoky Mountains National Park are protected from logging and other commercial activities within its boundaries, air pollution from outside the park continues to pose an ecological threat. Wind currents carry pollutants from urban areas, industrial sites, and power plants into the park, where the tall mountains and local weather patterns trap and concentrate the man-made pollutants. Over the past fifty years, the air quality in the park has declined significantly. A whitish haze often obscures the scenic views and threatens the health of plants and animals within the park as well as the health of park visitors.

A 1977 amendment to the federal Clean Air Act designated all national parks over 6,000 acres as mandatory Class I areas worthy of the greatest degree of air quality protection under the Act. Federal land managers (employees of the Department of the Interior) are instructed to take an aggressive role to "protect air-quality related values" including visibility, flora, fauna, surface water, ecosystems, and historic resources. The National Park Service now comments on state air quality permit applications for major factories, power plants, and other air pollution sources proposed for location near national parks. This has helped curb the construction of new pollution sources. However, in 2017, when the administration appointed Scott Pruitt to the Environmental Protection Agency and Ryan Zinke to the Department of the Interior, they gave a clear message that industry was to be favored over environment. It is our job to speak out and demand that our wild places be protected.

"Gathering of Souls" Synchronous Fireflies in Great Smoky Mountains National Park; Photo: ©Radim Schreiber Please see more of Radim's wonderful photography at http://www.fireflyexperience.org

SYNCHRONOUS FIREFLY

Synchronous Firefly was designed to show off beautifully dyed worsted weight yarn. It features an undulating wave pattern with large sections of stockinette stitch punctuated by graceful lines of yarn overs. The cowl is knit in the round and works up quickly. The mitts feature the wave pattern on the cuff and the back of the hand.

SIZES
One size

FINISHED MEASUREMENTS:
Cowl: 22 inches / 55.75 cm circumference X 8.5 inches / 21.5 cm tall
Mitts: Hand circumference 7 inches / 17.75 cm

MATERIALS
Yarn: Knit Picks Preciosa Tonal (100% merino wool; 273 yards/100 grams); color: Bonsai; mitts 100 yards: cowl 165 yards (1 skein makes both)

Needles: Cowl - 24 inch US#8 / 5 mm circular needle, or size needed to obtain gauge
Mitts - set of 5 US#8 / 5 mm double pointed needles, or size needed to obtain gauge

Stitch marker
Stitch holder or scrap yarn
Tapestry needle

GAUGE
18 sts and 28 rnds = 4 inches in stockinette stitch

SPECIAL STITCHES AND TECHNIQUES

Stretchy bind off: K2, place tip of LH needle into fronts of these 2 sts, k2tog, *k1, place tip of LH needle into fronts of these 2 sts, k2tog, rep from * until all sts have been bound off.

PATTERN

Cowl

With the circular needle, CO 105 sts and join in the round taking care not to twist the stitches. Place a marker at the end of the rnd. (For a wider cowl, cast on additional sts in multiples of 7.)

Rnds 1, 3, and 5: Purl.

Rnds 2, 4, and 6: Knit.

Rnd 7: *K5, k2tog, yo; rep from * to end of rnd.

Rnd 8 and all even rnds (except as noted): Knit.

Rnd 9: *K4, k2tog, k1, yo; rep from * to end of rnd.

Rnd 11: *K3, k2tog, k2, yo; rep from * to end of rnd.

Rnd 13: *K2, k2tog, k3, yo; rep from * to end of rnd.

Rnd 15: *K1, k2tog, k4, yo; rep from * to end of rnd.

Rnd 17: *K2tog, k5, yo; rep from * to end of rnd.

Rnd 19: *K2, yo, ssk, k3; rep from * to end of rnd.

Rnd 21: *K2, yo, k1, ssk, k2; rep from * to end of rnd.

Rnd 23: *K2, yo, k2, ssk, k1; rep from * to end of rnd.

Rnd 25: *K2, yo, k3, ssk; rep from * to end of rnd.

Rnd 27: Sl 1st st of rnd (now the last st of rnd), *k1, yo, k4, ssk; rep from * to end of rnd.

Rnd 29: Sl 1st st of rnd (now the last st of rnd), *yo, k5, ssk; rep from * to end of rnd.

Rnd 30: Knit to last 2 sts. This is the new end of rnd.

Rep rnds 7 - 30 one more time (or more for a taller cowl.)

Rep rnds 1 - 6 one time.

BO all sts using the stretchy bind off.

Weave in loose ends.

Block gently.

Mitts

Cuff (Both hands)

With the DPNs, CO 28 sts evenly across 4 needles. Join in the round taking care not to twist the work.

Rnds 1, 3, and 5: Purl.

Rnds 2, 4, and 6: Knit.

Rnd 7: *K5, k2tog, yo; rep from * to end of rnd.

Rnd 8 and all even rnds except as noted: Knit.

Rnd 9: *K4, k2tog, k1, yo; rep from * to end of rnd.

Rnd 11: *K3, k2tog, k2, yo; rep from * to end of rnd.

Rnd 13: *K2, k2tog, k3, yo; rep from * to end of rnd.

Rnd 15: *K1, k2tog, k4, yo; rep from * to end of rnd.

Rnd 17: *K2tog, k5, yo; rep from * to end of rnd.
Rnd 19: *K2, yo, ssk, k3; rep from * to end of rnd.
Rnd 21: *K2, yo, k1, ssk, k2; rep from * to end of rnd.
Rnd 23: *K2, yo, k2, ssk, k1; rep from * to end of rnd.
Rnd 25: *K2, yo, k3, ssk; rep from * to end of rnd.
Rnd 27: Sl 1st st of rnd (now the last st of rnd), *k1, yo, k4, ssk; rep from * to end of rnd.
Rnd 29: Sl 1st st of rnd (now the last st of rnd), *yo, k5, ssk; rep from * to end of rnd.
Rnd 30: Knit to last 2 sts. This is the new end of rnd.

Hand (Right)
Rnd 31: [K5, k2tog, yo] twice, m1, k14. - 29 sts.
Rnd 33: [K4, k2tog, k1, yo] twice, m1, k1, yo, k14. - 31 sts
Rnd 35: [K3, k2tog, k2, yo] twice, m1, k3, yo, k14. - 33 sts
Rnd 37: [K2, k2tog, k3, yo] twice, m1, k5, yo, k14. - 35 sts
Rnd 39: [K1, k2tog, k4, yo] three times, k14.
Rnd 41: [K2tog, k5, yo] three times, k14.
Rnd 42: K14, k7 and place these on scrap yarn, k14.
Rnd 43: [K2, yo, ssk, k3] twice, CO2, k14. - 30 sts
Rnd 45: [K2, yo, k1, ssk, k2] twice, k16.
Rnd 47: [K2, yo, k2, ssk, k1] twice, k16.
Rnd 49: [K2, yo, k3, ssk] twice, k16.
Rnd 51: Sl 1st st of rnd (now the last st of rnd), [k1, yo, k4, ssk] twice, k16.
Rnd 53: Sl 1st st of rnd (now the last st of rnd), [yo, k5, ssk] twice, k16.
Rnd 54: Knit.
Rep rnds 1 - 6 one time.
BO all sts using the stretchy bind off.

Hand (Left)
Rnd 31: K14, m1, [k5, k2tog, yo] twice. - 29 sts
Rnd 33: K14, m1, k1, yo, [k4, k2tog, k1, yo] twice. - 31 sts
Rnd 35: K14, m1, k3, yo, [k3, k2tog, k2, yo] twice. - 33 sts
Rnd 37: K14, m1, k5, yo, [k2, k2tog, k3, yo] twice. -35 sts
Rnd 39: K14, [k1, k2tog, k4, yo] three times.
Rnd 41: K14, [k2tog, k5, yo] three times.
Rnd 42: K14, k7 and place these on scrap yarn, k14.
Rnd 43: K14, CO2, [k2, yo, ssk, k3] twice. - 30 sts
Rnd 45: K16, [k2, yo, k1, ssk, k2] twice.
Rnd 47: K16, [k2, yo, k2, ssk, k1] twice.
Rnd 49: K16, [k2, yo, k3, ssk] twice.
Rnd 51: Sl 1st st of rnd (now the last st of rnd), k16, [k1, yo, k4, ssk] twice.
Rnd 53: Sl 1st st of rnd (now the last st of rnd), k16, [yo, k5, ssk] twice.
Rnd 54: Knit.
Rep rnds 1 - 6 one time.
BO all sts using the stretchy bind off.

Thumb (Both hands)
Place the 7 sts from the scrap yarn onto 2 dpns. With a third dpn, pick up 2 sts from the CO edge at the hand. - 9 sts
Rep rnds 19 - 25 once, working the 2 picked up sts as knits in all rnds.

Next rnd: Knit.
Rep rnds 1 - 6 once.
BO all sts using the stretchy bind off.

Weave in loose ends.
Block gently.

Staring Contest with a Green Frog at the Ipswich River Wildlife Sanctuary
Photo: ©Samuel Silver

GLACIER NATIONAL PARK

In 1910, President Taft created Glacier National Park in northern Montana, making it our 10th national park. This massive park of over one million acres includes parts of two mountain ranges. Within the park are over 700 bodies of water, 734 miles of hiking trails, and thousands of plant and animal species. The abundance of large mammals, such as elk, moose, grizzly bears, lynx, and wolverines, contributes to a feeling of untamed wilderness. Glacier National Park is one of the last places in this country where visitors can get a glimpse of what much of the west was like before the industrial revolution gave us the cacophony of modern life that we know today.

The imposing vistas and landscapes of Glacier National Park were carved out by the massive glaciers that give the park its name. The glaciers in the park are estimated to be approximately 7,000 years old. They reached their maximum size during a period known as the "little ice age" approximately 300–400 years ago. The glaciers have been naturally receding since then, but the process has sped up significantly in recent years. This is likely yet one more effect of human caused climate change on our planet. While glaciers can still be seen today, they have shrunk noticeably since the park's formation. Current data suggest that the last glaciers will be gone from the park by 2030.

Since 1992, Glacier National Park has served as a prime research location for scientists concerned about climate change and its effects on fragile alpine ecosystems. Researchers are studying changes in forest fire patterns and how the forest ecology reacts to those changes. They monitor changes in alpine vegetation patterns and track stream flow rates and temperatures. Atmospheric monitoring stations measure UV-B radiation, ozone and other atmospheric gases over time. This wealth of data combined with similar efforts from around the world is helping researchers piece together a picture of the effects of climatic change on a global scale.

McDonald Lake Valley Viewed from the South Shore of McDonald Lake, Glacier National Park, Montana; Photo: ©Melinda Ratchye

"I often wonder at the awesome power behind the glacier that created this valley and am grateful to experience the calming peace that envelops the breathtaking mountains and serene crystal clear lakes. It is a tradition for my little family to come here every year. Even after fires have swept through it never disappoints, and we always see something new and magical."

GLACIER

Glacier is a monolithic stockinette stitch crescent shawl with a delicate water drop pattern lace dripping from the edge. Pick a soft, cozy yarn for the main body of the shawl that will be a pleasure to knit. Use silk for the lace edge to add shine.

SIZES
One size (Size is adjustable depending on amount of yarn used. Sample shown uses nearly all of 2 skeins of the heavier yarn.)

FINISHED MEASUREMENTS
Length 88 inches / 223.5 cm
Width 23 inches / 58.5 cm

MATERIALS
Heavier yarn: Knit Picks Diadem Fingering (50% baby alpaca, 50% mulberry silk; 329 yards/100 grams); color: Pearl Solid; 2 skeins
Lighter yarn: Knit Picks Luminance (100% silk; 439 yards/100 grams); color: Reflection; 1 skein

Needles: 40 inch US #7 / 4.5mm circular needle, or size needed to obtain gauge

Tapestry needle

GAUGE
16 sts and 32 rows = 4 inches / 10 cm in stockinette stitch using heavier yarn

SPECIAL STITCHES AND TECHNIQUES

Kyok (knit, yarn over, knit): Knit, then yo, then knit again into the same stitch. Three sts made from 1 st.

Pk (purl, knit): Purl then knit into the same stitch. Two sts made from 1 st.

Stretchy bind off: K2, place tip of LH needle into fronts of these 2 sts, k2tog, *k1, place tip of LH needle into fronts of these 2 sts, k2tog, rep from * until all sts have been bound off.

PATTERN

Body

With heavier yarn, CO 6 sts.

Row 1 (WS): K2, yo, k2, yo, k2.

Row 2 (RS): K2, kyok, k2, kyok, k2.

Row 3: K2, yo, k8, yo, k2.

Row 4: K2, kyok, k8, kyok, k2.

Row 5: K2, yo, purl to last 2 sts, yo, k2.

Row 6: K2, kyok, knit to last 3 sts, kyok, k2.

Rep rows 5 and 6 until the shawl body is the desired size.

Row 7: *Yo, p2tog; rep from * to end of row.

Cut yarn.

Edge

With lighter yarn.

Row 8: *K1, kyok; rep from * to end of row.

Row 9: P2, *yo, p4; rep from * to last 2 sts, yo, p2.

Row 10: Ssk, *pk, k2tog, ssk; rep from * to last 3 sts, pk, k2tog.

Row 11: P4, *yo, p4; rep from * to end of row.

Row 12: K2, ssk, *pk, k2tog, ssk; rep from * to last 5 sts, pk, k2tog, k2.

Rep rows 9 - 12 four more times (five reps total.)

BO all sts using the stretchy bind off.

Weave in loose ends.

Block well to form curved shape and to open the lace.

John Muir and the Sierra Club

"Poetico-trampo-geologist-botanist and ornithologist-naturalist etc. etc. !!!!" is how John Muir (1838-1914) once described himself. He was a devoted naturalist and conservationist. While his adventures took him to a variety of places, including Alaska's Glacier Bay, he is best known for his time spent exploring and writing about California's Sierra Nevada mountain range.

John Muir was devoted to the cause of preserving the pristine wild places. In 1890, Muir helped lobby Congress for the act that created Yosemite National Park. But the park remained under state control until 1906, when Muir convinced President Roosevelt to sign a bill that transferred the park to federal control. His words and actions helped inspire President Theodore Roosevelt's other conservation programs. Muir's work ultimately led to the formation of Sequoia, Mount Rainier, Petrified Forest, and Grand Canyon National Parks.

John Muir's vision carries on through the work of the Sierra Club. Founded in 1892 by John and his supporters, it is the Sierra Club's mission to explore, enjoy, and protect the wild places. Over the years they have protected millions of acres of wilderness. They helped pass the Clean Air Act, the Clean Water Act, and the Endangered Species Act. Today, the Sierra Club can be found on the front lines of conservation, fighting to protect America's public lands, educating about the effects of fossil fuels on the environment, and providing opportunities for people to explore and enjoy the natural world.

I will be donating 5% of my profits from *Knitting Wild* to the Sierra Club to help them continue their work and carry on John Muir's legacy.

Grand Canyon National Park; Photo: ©Elizabeth Fisher

"This rock formation captures what I love most about the Grand Canyon. Each rock layer has its own character, due not only to its color and texture, but also to the plants making their home there. Here, the prominent Redwall limestone contrasts with the dark green of the juniper trees growing in its crevasses. The Tonto Group, forming softer slopes below in yellow and brown, is more harmonious with its blanket of grey-green sage."

PETRIFIED FOREST NATIONAL PARK

Petrified Forest National Park in Arizona started as one of the first national monuments created under the 1906 Antiquities Act, signed by President Theodore Roosevelt. The act gives the president the power to create national monuments from federal land to protect significant natural, cultural, or scientific features. In the case of Petrified Forest, the designation was made to protect the massive deposit of petrified trees found on the land from theft and damage. Over time the monument was enlarged to include a section of the Painted Desert, and in 1962 it was converted into a national park. Since 1906 the Antiquities Act has been used by nearly every sitting president to protect land sacred to Native Americans as well as locations of biological importance. In 2017, for the first time ever, the president reduced the size of existing monuments, cutting Bears Ears and Grand Staircase–Escalante Monuments to fractions of their original sizes.

While Petrified Forest National Park takes its name from the vast cache of petrified wood it protects, it also contains a wealth of other paleontological, archaeological, and biological information to be discovered and studied. Paleontologists come from all over the world to study the rich fossil record, reconstructing ancient environments and uncovering information about climate change in the past that may help us understand its effects today. Archaeologists are able to study hundreds of sites of early human habitation dating back as far as 13,000 years. Biologists study the fragile desert ecosystems, the animals that live there, and the effects environmental change has on them. Recent expansion of the park has opened up vast new areas for these scientists to explore, enhancing our understanding of the planet today and in the past.

In the northern section of Petrified Forest National Park are the arid badlands known as the Painted Desert. The harsh landscape has been heavily eroded, exposing a rainbow of vividly colored sedimentary layers. These layers of siltstone, mudstone, and shale make up the Triassic Chinle Formation. The variety of colors are the result of mineral oxides within the layers of sediment. At times when the layers were built up slowly, extensive oxidation occurred, creating vivid red, yellow, and orange colors.

When sediment was deposited quickly, such as in a flood, the layers were deprived of oxygen and blue, lavender, and grey colors result. As hillsides are eroded away, a multi-colored history lesson is revealed. Each layer tells its own story about the environmental conditions present when it was formed. Each layer also yields a treasure trove of plant and animal fossils that can be placed into this environmental context, furthering our understanding of the forces that have shaped life on Earth.

Great Horned Owl, Saguaro National Park, Arizona; Photo: ©Marilyn Barnes

"This handsome fellow is part of a raptor show at the Arizona/Sonora Desert Museum. All birds used in the show are not tethered and are free to leave at any time. He is posing in his natural habitat."

PAINTED DESERT

The painted desert cowl and mitts use a series of slip stitch rows to create layers of color. Both pieces are knit in the round. The mitts include a gusset thumb. The colorwork is simple, using only one yarn per round, making it a great first project for someone who has never done colorwork before.

SIZES
One Size

FINISHED MEASUREMENTS
Cowl: 29 inches / 73.75 cm circumference X 12 inches / 30.5 cm tall
Mitts: hand circumference 6.5 inches / 16.5 cm (unstretched)

MATERIALS
Yarn: Knit Picks Preciosa Tonal (100% merino wool; 273 yards/100 grams); cowl 390 yards, mitts 190 yards; colors:
A: Gladiola, B: Boysenberry, C: Duchess, D: Anemone, E: Canary

Needles: 24 inch US #8 / 5mm circular needle, or size needed to obtain gauge
Set of 5 US #8 / 5mm double pointed needles, or size needed to obtain gauge

Stitch marker
Stitch holder or scrap yarn
Tapestry needle

GAUGE
16 st and 24 rnds = 4 inches / 10 cm in stockinette stitch

Pattern Notes

Lay out your color progression before you begin knitting. As shown the cowl and mitts have 17 stripes in the following progression:

A B C D E D C B A B C D E D C B A

Do not twist the bar when working the m1 increases; lift the bar between sts onto the LH needle and knit into the FRONT of the bar.

Each time you work a rep of the body section you will be working with only two colors. The first time through "previous color" is A and "next color" is B. In the second repeat, "previous color" is B and "next color" is C, etc.

Special Stitches and Techniques

Stretchy bind off: K2, place tip of LH needle into fronts of these 2 sts, k2tog, *k1, place tip of LH needle into fronts of these 2 sts, k2tog, rep from * until all sts have been bound off.

Cowl

Set-Up

With first color and 24 inch circular needle, CO 120 sts and join in the round taking care not to twist the stitches. Place a marker at the end of the rnd.

Rnds 1 and 3: Knit.
Rnds 2 and 4: Purl.
Rnds 5 and 6: Knit.

Body

Switch to next color.
Rnd 7: *Sl1, m1; rep from * to end of rnd.
Switch to previous color.
Rnd 8: *K1, sl1; rep from * to end of rnd.
Switch to next color.
Rnd 9: *Sl1, k1; rep from * to end of rnd.
Switch to previous color.
Rnd 10: *K1, sl1; rep from * to end of rnd.
Switch to next color and cut previous color.
Rnd 11: *K2tog; rep from * to end of rnd.
Rnds 12 and 13: Knit.
Rep body section until all colors in the sequence have been worked ending with rnd 11 of the last rep.

Finish

With last color:
Rnds 14 and 16: Purl.
Rnds 15 and 17: Knit.
BO all sts using the stretchy bind off.

Weave in loose ends.
Block gently.

Mitts

Cuff

Set-Up

With first color and set of DPNs, CO 34 sts distributed 6 sts on the 1st, 2nd, and 3rd needles, and 16 sts on the 4th needle. Join in the round taking care not to twist the stitches.

Rnds 1 and 3: Knit.
Rnds 2 and 4: Purl.
Rnd 5: Knit.
Rnd 6: Knit to last 2 sts, k2tog.
Switch to next color.
Rnd 7: *Sl1, m1; rep from * to end of rnd.
Switch to previous color.
Rnd 8: *K1, sl1; rep from * to end of rnd.
Switch to next color.
Rnd 9: *Sl1, k1; rep from * to end of rnd.
Switch to previous color.
Rnd 10: *K1, sl1; rep from * to end of rnd.
Switch to next color and cut previous color.
Rnd 11: *K2tog; rep from * to end of rnd.
Rnd 12: Knit.
Rnd 13: Knit to last 2 sts, k2tog. - 1 st removed
Rep rnds 7 - 13 eight more times.
You will have 10 stripes and 24 sts.
Place a marker after the 11th stitch.

Gusset

Switch to next color.
Rnd 14: *Sl1, m1; rep from * to end of rnd. (Work the m1 before slipping the marker.)
Switch to previous color.

Rnd 15: *K1, sl1; rep from * to end of rnd.
Switch to next color.
Rnd 16: *Sl1, k1; rep from * to end of rnd.
Switch to previous color.
Rnd 17: *K1, sl1; rep from * to end of rnd.
Switch to next color and cut previous color.
Rnd 18: *K2tog; rep from * to 2 sts before the marker, k2, slm, k2tog, k2tog, k2, *k2tog; rep from * to end of rnd. - 2 sts added
Rnd 19 and 20: Knit.
Rep rnds 14 - 20 two more times. You will have 13 stripes and 30 sts.
Switch to next color. (You can now remove the marker.)
Rnd 21: *Sl1, m1; rep from * to end of rnd.
Switch to previous color.
Rnd 22: *K1, sl1; rep from * to end of rnd.
Switch to next color.
Rnd 23: *Sl1, k1; rep from * to end of rnd.
Switch to previous color.
Rnd 24: *K1, sl1; rep from * to end of rnd.
Switch to next color and cut previous color.
Rnd 25: *K2tog; rep from * to end of rnd.
Rnd 26: Knit.
Rnd 27: K12, place the next 6 sts on

scrap yarn, using backwards loop method CO 2 sts, k12.
You will have 14 stripes and 26 sts.

Hand
Switch to next color.
Rnd 28: *Sl1, m1; rep from * to end of rnd.
Switch to previous color.
Rnd 29: *K1, sl1; rep from * to end of rnd.
Switch to next color.
Rnd 30: *Sl1, k1; rep from * to end of rnd.
Switch to previous color.
Rnd 31: *K1, sl1; rep from * to end of rnd.
Switch to next color and cut previous color.
Rnd 32: *K2tog; rep from * to end of rnd.
Rnd 33 and 34: Knit.
Rep rnds 28 - 34 one more time. You will have 16 stripes.
Rep rnds 28 - 32 one more time.
Rnds 35 and 37: Purl.
Rnds 36 and 38: Knit.
BO all sts using the stretchy bind off.

Thumb
Place 6 sts from the scrap yarn onto needles.
With previous color, pick up 2 sts from the CO edge at the hand.
Rnd 1: Knit.
Switch to next color.
Rnd 2: *Sl1, m1; rep from * to end of rnd.
Switch to previous color.
Rnd 3: *K1, sl1; rep from * to end of rnd.

Switch to next color.
Rnd 4: *Sl1, k1; rep from * to end of rnd.
Switch to previous color.
Rnd 5: *K1, sl1; rep from * to end of rnd.
Switch to next color and cut previous color.
Rnd 6: *K2tog; rep from * to end of rnd.
Rnds 7 and 9: Purl.
Rnds 8 and 10: Knit.
BO all sts using the stretchy bind off.

Weave in loose ends.
You will need to use a tail to close the hole where the thumb meets the hand.
Block gently.

Repeat for second mitt.

Lassen Volcanic National Park

Lassen Volcanic National Park in Northern California protects a little over 100,000 acres of geologically active landscape. Parts of the park had previously been protected as preserves and monuments as early as 1907. However, the park was formally established in 1916 when a series of eruptions on Mt Lassen sparked renewed interest in the area. In addition to its geological features, the park provides habitat for an array of plants and animals. Visitors come to hike and camp in its wild beauty.

Lassen Volcanic National Park includes the southernmost volcano in the Cascade range, Mt. Lassen, as well as an assortment of other active volcanoes and geothermal features. Superheated water seeps up through the ground, forming bubbling mud pots and hot springs, while sulphurous steam works its way through porous rock formations to create hissing, steaming fumaroles. Today the park offers visitors a fascinating peek into the volcanic history of the Cascade mountain range, which has shaped so much of the Pacific Northwest. It also provides a vast laboratory for geologists, hydrologists, and biologists.

Snowpack from the Cascades and the Sierra Nevadas (south of the park) provide over a third of California's water. Lassen Volcanic National Park alone contains four watersheds fed by snowpack from Mt Lassen. Historically, water fell as snow in the mountains through much of the year. It accumulated and was stored in the form of snowpack. In the summer the water was slowly released as the snow melted, providing water to lower elevations during otherwise dry times of the year. However, rising temperatures due to global climate change are causing more precipitation to fall as rain and the snowpack that does form begins to melt earlier in the year. Lassen Volcanic National Park provides a place for scientists to study how the changes in snowpack affect ecosystems within the park and beyond. It also serves as a place for hydrologists to develop the new technology to capture and store water that will be needed in the future.

Bighorn Sheep in Glacier National Park; Photo: ©Samuel Silver

Fumarole

Fumarole is a fun, slouchy hat. The allover pattern of yarnovers gives a delicate, airy look and keeps it from being too heavy. Knit from the top down of worsted weight yarn, this is a quick, easy project.

Sizes
One Size

Finished Measurements
Band Circumference 18 inches / 45.75 cm (unstretched)

Materials
Yarn: Knit Picks Chroma Worsted (70% superwash wool, 30% nylon; 198 yards/100 grams); color: Manzanita; 1 skein

Needles: Set of 5 US #8 / 5mm double pointed needles, or size needed to obtain gauge

Stitch marker
Tapestry needle

Gauge
16 sts and 26 rnds = 4 inches / 10 cm in stockinette stitch

Pattern Notes

This hat is knit top down, which means it starts with just a few cast-on stitches. An i-cord technique for the first row is used to help prevent twisting.

Special Stitches and Techniques

Kyok (knit, yarn over, knit): Knit, then yo, then knit again into the the same st. Three sts made from 1 st.

Stretchy bind off: K2, place tip of LH needle into fronts of these 2 sts, k2tog, *k1, place tip of LH needle into fronts of these 2 sts, k2tog; rep from * until all sts have been bound off.

Pattern

Crown

CO 8 sts onto one needle.

Rnd 1: Starting with the first cast on stitch and bringing the working yarn across the back as for an i-cord, knit 2 sts onto the first dpn, switch to the second dpn and k2. Continue adding dpns until all the stitches have been worked and are distributed 2 sts per needle.

Rnd 2: *Yo, k1; rep from * to end of rnd. - 16 sts

Rnd 3: *Kyok, k1; rep from * to end

of rnd. - 32 sts

Rnd 4: *P3tog, k1; rep from * to end of rnd. - 16 sts

Rnds 5 & 6: Knit all sts.

Rep rnds 2 - 6 two more times (three reps total.) - 64 sts.

Rnd 7: *Yo, k1; rep from * to end of rnd.

Rnd 8: *Kyok, k1; rep from * to end of rnd.

Rnd 9: *P3tog, k1; rep from * to end of rnd.

Rnd 10: Knit all sts.

Rnd 11: *K2tog; rep from * to end of rnd.

Rep rnds 7 -1 1 five more times (six reps total), ending with rnd 10 in the last repeat.

Next Rnd: *[K2tog] seven times, k2; rep from * to end of rnd. - 72 sts.

Work 2.5 inches / 7.5 cm even in stockinette st.

BO all sts using the stretchy bind off.

Weave in loose ends.
Block gently to shape.

CAPE MEARES NATIONAL WILDLIFE REFUGE

Cape Meares National Wildlife Refuge was established in 1938 to protect one of the last stands of old growth forest on the Oregon Coast. Sitka spruce and Western Hemlock are the dominant species in this ancient forest ecosystem. These giant trees play host to the rare marbled murrelet. Unlike the rest of its alcid relatives, such as puffins and murres who nest on coastal cliffs and rocky islands, the murrelets build their nests high up in old growth trees. Loss of suitable old growth nesting habitat to logging has caused significant population decline in murrelets, resulting in their designation as a threatened species. The refuge also includes dramatic coastal cliffs where murres, guillemots, cormorants, and other seabirds nest. A platform overlooking the cliffs is an excellent spot for viewing the refuge's pair of peregrine falcons who raise chicks on the steep cliffs. Harbor seals, Steller sea lions, and California sea lions can be seen lounging on the rocks just offshore.

The Cape Meares Wildlife Refuge protects coastal shrublands and forest, including the most northerly stand of old-growth Sitka spruce remaining on the Oregon coast. Because of its pristine condition, the refuge is designated a Research Natural Area, meaning that natural processes are allowed to continue without interference. Activities within the refuge are limited to research, study, observation, monitoring, and education, and must be non-destructive, non-manipulative, and maintain unmodified conditions. Within this untouched landscape is a rich variety of life. The understory includes salal, salmonberry, sword fern, deer fern, evergreen huckleberry, and oxalis. Assorted small mammals, including at least eleven species of rodent, two of moles, and four of shrews, find food and nesting sites among the trees or in the understory. Seven species of salamander and two species of frogs inhabit the numerous bogs and marshes, or make homes under rotting, windfallen trees.

An old growth forest is far more than a group of really old trees. It is a highly complex, deeply interconnected ecosystem. The key component of an old growth forest is time. Over the course of several hundred years, complexity builds up as generations live, die, and decompose. This endless cycle creates layers and interdependencies that cannot be replicated in the young monoculture forests that result from replanting after clearcutting.

Decay is a vital part of the old growth forest ecosystem. But decay doesn't just happen. It is an active process carried out by organisms, collectively called decomposers, that feed off dead material, breaking it down and ultimately releasing its nutrients back into the environment. One of the most important decomposers in an old growth forest is shelf or bracket fungi. These fungi are characterized by the production of fruiting bodies called "conks." These shelf shaped structures can be found growing on dead and dying trees. But the conks represent only a small portion of the fungus. The rest of the fungus is inside the tree, breaking down the wood and ultimately creating the rich soil in which the next generation of trees will grow. In many species, conks are perennial, adding new layers of growth each year.

Adult Marbled Murrelet; Photo: Roy W. Lowe, U.S. Fish and Wildlife Service

Conks

Conks is an unusually shaped shawlette that starts small and grows in layers of stockinette stitch interspersed with sections of garter stitch. The increases are biased toward the beginning of each row to create an asymmetrical curve. The shawl starts with just a few stitches and gets larger with each pattern repeat, allowing the knitter to easily customize the finished size. It is the perfect project for that treasured skein of sock yarn in your stash.

Sizes
One Size (Size is adjustable depending on amount of yarn used. Sample shown uses the entire skein of yarn.)

Finished Measurements
Length 40 inches / 101.5 cm

Materials
Yarn: Knit Picks Hawthorne Fingering (80% superwash wool, 20% polyamide; 357 yards/100 grams); color: Lovejoy; 1 skein

Needles: US #6 / 4mm circular needle, or size needed to obtain gauge

Tapestry needle

Gauge
22 sts and 28 rows = 4 inches / 10 cm in stockinette stitch

PATTERN

Set-Up

CO 2 sts.

Row 1 (WS): Knit.

Row 2 (RS): K1, m1, k1. - 3 sts

Row 3: Knit.

Row 4: [K1, m1] twice, k1. - 5 sts

Rows 5 - 7: Knit.

Row 8: [K1, m1] twice, k2, m1, k1. - 8 sts

Rows 9 - 13: Knit.

Main Body

1st Inc Row: [K1, m1] twice, [k2, m1] twice, k2. - 12 sts

Rows 2, 4, and 6: K1, purl to end of row.

Rows 3, 5, and 7: Knit.

Rows 8 - 12: Knit.

2nd Inc Row: [K1, m1] twice, [k2, m1] twice, k3, m1, k3. - 17 sts

Work rows 2 - 12.

3rd Inc Row: [K1, m1] twice, [k2,

m1] twice, [k3, m1] twice, k4, m1, k1. - 24 sts.
Work rows 2 - 12.

Continue in the established pattern working increase rows as follows:

4th Inc Row: [K1, m1] twice, [k2, m1] twice, [k3, m1] twice, [k4, m1] twice, k4. - 32 sts

5th Inc Row: [K1, m1] twice, [k2, m1] twice, [k3, m1] twice, [k4, m1] twice, [k5, m1] twice, k2. - 42 sts

6th Inc Row: [K1, m1] twice, [k2, m1] twice, [k3, m1] twice, [k4, m1] twice, [k5, m1] twice, [k6, m1] twice. - 54 sts

7th Inc Row: [K1, m1] twice, [k2, m1] twice, [k3, m1] twice, [k4, m1] twice, [k5, m1] twice, [k6, m1] twice, k7, m1, k5. - 67 sts

8th Inc Row: [K1, m1] twice, [k2, m1] twice, [k3, m1] twice, [k4, m1] twice, [k5, m1] twice, [k6, m1] twice, [k7, m1] twice, k8, m1, k3. - 82 sts

9th Inc Row: [K1, m1] twice, [k2, m1] twice, [k3, m1] twice, [k4, m1] twice, [k5, m1] twice, [k6, m1] twice, [k7, m1] twice, [k8, m1] twice, k9, m1, k1. - 99 sts

10th Inc Row: [K1, m1] twice, [k2, m1] twice, [k3, m1] twice, [k4, m1] twice, [k5, m1] twice, [k6, m1] twice, [k7, m1] twice, [k8, m1] twice, [k9, m1] twice, k9. - 117 sts

11th Inc Row: [K1, m1] twice, [k2, m1] twice, [k3, m1] twice, [k4, m1] twice, [k5, m1] twice, [k6, m1] twice, [k7, m1] twice, [k8, m1] twice, [k9, m1] twice, [k10, m1] twice, k7. - 137 sts

12th Inc Row: [K1, m1] twice, [k2, m1] twice, [k3, m1] twice, [k4, m1] twice, [k5, m1] twice, [k6, m1] twice, [k7, m1] twice, [k8, m1] twice, [k9, m1] twice, [k10, m1] twice, [k11, m1] twice, k5. - 159 sts

13th Inc Row: [K1, m1] twice, [k2, m1] twice, [k3, m1] twice, [k4, m1] twice, [k5, m1] twice, [k6, m1] twice, [k7, m1] twice, [k8, m1] twice, [k9, m1] twice, [k10, m1] twice, [k11, m1] twice, [k12, m1] twice, k3. - 183 sts

14th Inc Row: [K1, m1] twice, [k2, m1] twice, [k3, m1] twice, [k4, m1] twice, [k5, m1] twice, [k6, m1] twice, [k7, m1] twice, [k8, m1] twice, [k9, m1] twice, [k10, m1] twice, [k11, m1] twice, [k12, m1] twice, [k13, m1] twice, k1. - 209 sts

If a larger shawl is desired work additional reps of the body section. The basic increase sequence is:

[K1, m1] twice, [k2, m1] twice, [k3, m1] twice, [k4, m1] twice, [k5, m1] twice, etc.
Work as much of the sequence as fits in the row.

Bind off after row 12.

Weave in loose ends.
Block gently, taking care to create the curved shape.

Mushroom Gazing, Elk Knob State Park, NC
Photo: ©Knit Eco Chic by Lindsay Lewchuk

"You'd think hiking with senior citizens would mean spending a lot of time waiting and you're right. However, in my family, it's the seniors doing the waiting! Happily I am the butt of the family joke when it comes to hiking. Captivated by God's creativity I wander through the trails pausing frequently to snap a photo that's caught my eye while Puddles runs back and forth and my parents tease my speed. They've even threatened to take away my camera... but I have my cell as a back up. Once the destination is set, the journey is free to be enjoyed as much as possible! One of the elements most often found in my viewer, after a certain Great Dane, that is, are mushrooms. Our mountains are covered in this particular variety, which mostly grow on felled trees or stumps. "

ARCTIC NATIONAL WILDLIFE REFUGE

Encompassing over 19 million acres, Arctic National Wildlife Refuge is the largest refuge in the US. The land protected includes some of the harshest and most delicate landscapes on the planet. The mission of the refuge is to conserve animals and plants in their natural diversity, ensure a place for hunting and gathering activities, protect water quality and quantity, and fulfill international wildlife treaty obligations (most notably the migratory bird treaty). This is a broad mandate, and one that is increasingly hard to fulfill as human activities in other places on the planet create global effects.

The effects of climate change are seen throughout the refuge. Melting sea ice brings polar bears onshore, where they disrupt food chains by switching to new prey species. Plants on the refuge have a very short growing season, only 50-60 days, making them particularly vulnerable to climate disruptions. Changes to plant growth cycles in turn affect the growth and behavior patterns of the herbivores that rely on those plants.

Despite its harsh climate, the vast Arctic National Wildlife Refuge is home to a surprising array of fish, mammal, and bird species. Many of these animals migrate long distances to take advantage of the brief but productive arctic summer. Muskoxen, looking like they just stepped out of the last ice age with their stocky bodies and shaggy coats, are the only large mammal in the region to tough it out through the dark, frigid, nine month long winter. But more than 100 years ago the muskox had completely disappeared from the arctic landscape. It is only through reintroduction and habitat protection that they have returned to once again roam the frozen north. Whether they will continue to do so will be determined by the decisions we make in the coming decades.

While the land of the refuge is protected from commercial use, it was not really intended for recreational use either. Even minimal human activities in the region can have damaging effects on the landscape. There are no roads in the refuge, and while people may visit the area, their only options are to arrive by plane or to hike.

Today the refuge is caught in a tug-of-war between conservation and profit. Despite the mandate to protect the pristine wilderness, oil companies are again finding allies in the federal government. Whether this land and its inhabitants will be sacrificed for short term profits or preserved for future generations is one of the most pressing issues facing us today.

Denali National Park; Photo: ©Marilyn Barnes

Muskox

Muskox is a super bulky hat designed to keep you stylishly warm even on the coldest of days. The cabled band is knit flat and then joined. Stitches are picked up along the edge of the band and the rest of the hat is worked. The crown has a little extra fullness which gives it a slightly whimsical look.

SIZES
One Size

FINISHED MEASUREMENTS
Band Circumference 20 inches / 50.75 cm (unstretched)

MATERIALS
Yarn: Knit Picks The Big Cozy (55% superfine alpaca, 45% Peruvian highland wool; 44 yards/100 grams); color: Bittersweet Heather; 2 skeins

Needles: Set of 5 US #15 / 10 mm double pointed needles, or size needed to obtain gauge

Cable needle
Stitch markers
Tapestry needle

GAUGE
8 sts and 12 rows = 4 inches in seed stitch
NOTE: ROW gauge is more important for fit in this pattern

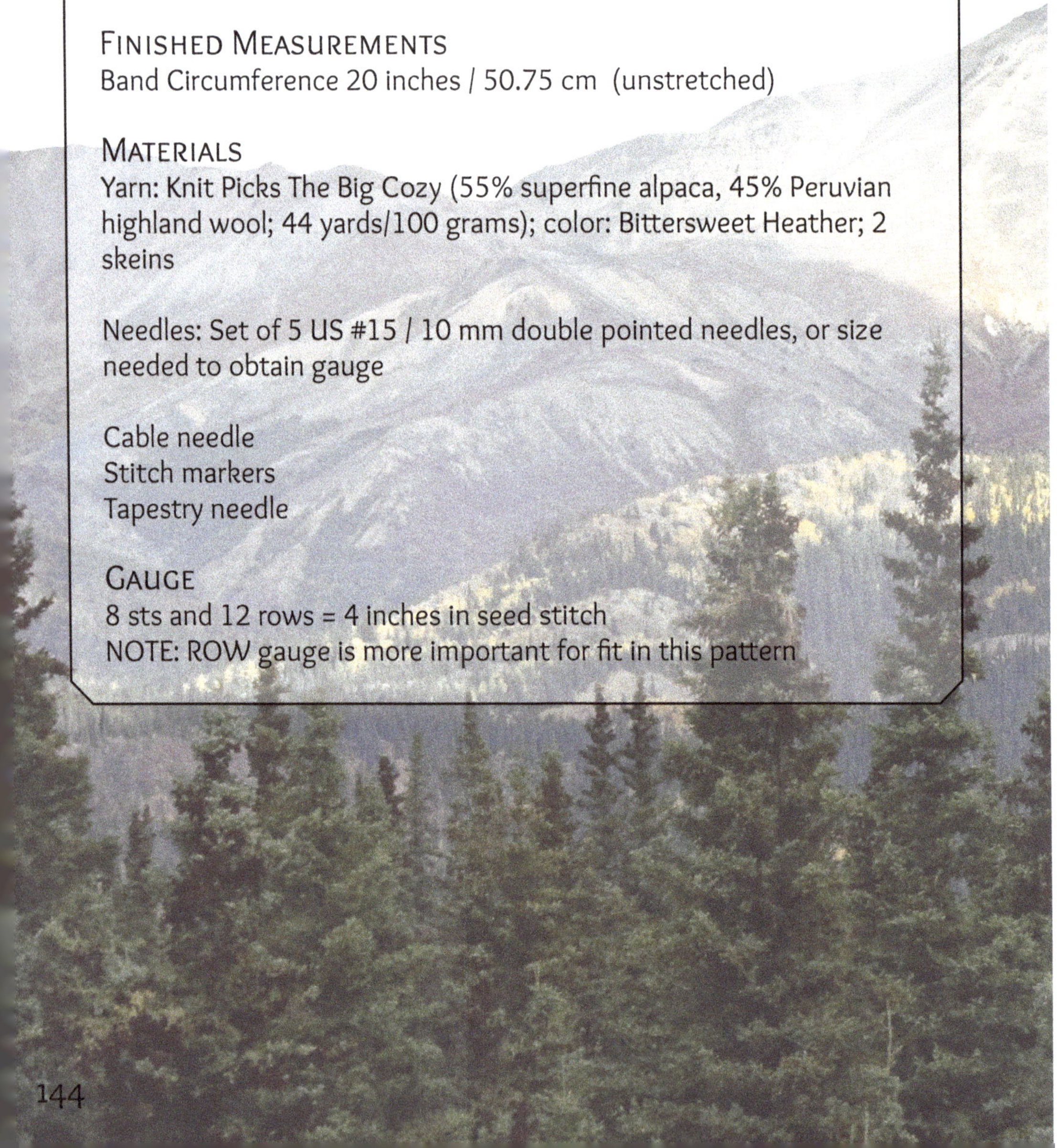

SPECIAL STITCHES AND TECHNIQUES

c4over4L (cable 4 over 4 left): Sl 4 sts onto cable needle, hold in front of work, k4, k4 from cable needle.

PATTERN
Brim
Using a provisional cast on, CO 16 sts.
Row 1: Knit.
Row 2 and all even rows (WS): Sl1 wyif, k1, p8, k2, [p1, k1] twice.
Row 3 (RS): [K1, p1] three times, k8, p1, k1.
Row 5: [K1, p1] three times, C4over4L, p1, k1.
Row 7: Rep row 3.

Rep rows 2 - 7 twelve more times (13 reps total.)

Open the provisional cast on and place the sts on a needle. Using your preferred grafting method join the two ends together to form a loop.

Crown
Working from the RS pick up 72 sts knitwise from the left selvedge edge, placing a marker every 9 sts.

Knit 3 rnds.
Dec Rnd: *Knit to 2 sts before marker, k2tog; rep from * to end of rnd. - 64 sts
Knit 2 rnds.
Work another decr rnd. - 56 sts
Knit 1 rnd.
Work decr every rnd until only 8 sts remain.
Cut the yarn.

Using a tapestry needle, thread the yarn through the remaining sts slipping them off the needle. Cinch the yarn to close the top of the hat.

Weave in the loose ends.
Block to shape.

Epilogue: Our Legacy of Abundance and Waste

The first European settlers in North America came to a land of almost unimaginable abundance. The ocean and rivers teemed with fish and the skies were darkened by flocks of ducks, geese, and other birds. The land itself appeared limitless, one game-filled acre after another, after another. This apparently endless supply of resources, combined with the religious belief in man's dominion over nature, led to indiscriminate use of these resources. Settlers cleared the land and harvested wildlife with no regard for future consequences.

Today, we have inherited that legacy. We live in increasingly homogeneous urban areas, mostly ignoring the natural world around us. Our lifestyle is fueled by resources that we don't even notice. We live a life filled with factory-produced abundance while ignoring the dwindling natural abundance. For over five hundred years we have treated the natural resources in this country as something to be owned, exploited, managed, and controlled. We have reached the tipping point. In the coming decades our actions will have profound effects not only on wildlife but also on the most vulnerable human populations. It is time to make some hard decisions. Are we willing to have less as individuals in order to have more for all living things?

Black Bear in Glacier National Park; Photo: ©Samuel Silver

Resources

Contact your elected officials
https://www.usa.gov/elected-officials

National Audubon Society
https://www.audubon.org

National Audubon info Page for their Migratory Bird Treaty Act Lawsuit
https://www.audubon.org/news/were-suing-federal-government-protect-birds

National Park Service
https://www.nps.gov/index.htm

National Resources Defense Council
https://www.nrdc.org

National Wildlife Refuges (U.S. Fish and Wildlife Service)
https://www.fws.gov/refuges/refugelocatormaps

Oaks Bottom Wildlife Refuge
https://www.portlandoregon.gov/parks/finder/index.cfm?propertyid=490&action=ViewPark

Project Puffin
http://projectpuffin.audubon.org

Reed College Canyon
https://www.reed.edu/canyon

Sierra Club
https://www.sierraclub.org

The Whooping Crane Eastern Partnership
https://www.bringbackthecranes.org

ABBREVIATIONS

b	bundle
BO	bind off
c4over4L	cable 4 over 4 left
cdd	central double decrease
CO	cast on
decr	decrease
dpn(s)	double pointed needle(s)
k	knit
K1tbl	knit 1 through the back loop
k2tog	knit 2 together
k3tog	knit 3 together
kfb	knit front and back
kyok	knit, yarn over, knit
LDI	lifted double increase
LH	left hand
LIL	lifted increase left
LIR	lifted increase right
m1	make 1 stitch
p	purl
p2tog	purl 2 together
p2togb	purl 2 together through the back loops
p3tog	purl 3 together
pk	purl knit
pm	place marker
psso	pass slipped stitch over

rep(s)	repeat(s)
rnd	round
RH	right hand
rm	remove marker
RS	right side
rt	right twist
sk2p	slip, knit 2 together, pass slipped stitch over
sl	slip
slm	slip marker
ssk	slip, slip, knit
st(s)	stitch(es)
WS	wrong side
wyif	with yarn in front
yo	yarn over

Wild Rose; Photo: ©Marilyn Barnes

Acknowledgments

This book would not have happened without the help, support, and contributions of the following folks. Thank you!

To Stephen Gerken, my husband and my editor, thank you for your love, your support, and your attention to detail.

To Marilyn Barnes, my photographer and my friend, thanks for being both.

To my lovely models, Chelsea Rinaldi, Lacy Schreiber, Reba Sparrow, and Robin Gill, thanks for being such good sports about getting up close and personal with nature.

To my sample knitters, Erica Stuart, Kate Lindstrom, Lilie Wells, and Mesha McMullen, thank you for your beautiful work.

To Knit Picks, who provided ALL the yarn, thank you for your generosity and support. It all knit up so beautifully.

To Reed College, thank you for letting us come on campus and take photos in the canyon. It's still one of my favorite places.

To Diana McIntosh and Louise Fisher, my cheerleaders, your constant interest and enthusiasm kept me going. Thanks for believing in me.

To all my Kickstarter donors, thank you for taking a risk on this project.

Photo Credits for Pattern Backgrounds

Howl (pg 16)
Yellowstone Lake; Photo: Author

Trillium (pg 30)
Crab Orchard Falls Trillium; Photo: ©Knit Eco Chic by Lindsay Lewchuk

Deciduous (pg 36)
Fall Foliage in East Greenbush; Photo: ©Gregory Polyakov

Cuyahoga Canals (pg 42)
Violetes in Cuyahoga Valley National Park; Photo © Meri Ruble

Whoop! Whoop! (pg 50)
Wild Rose; Photo: ©Marilyn Barnes

Pihemanu (pg 56)
U.S. Fish and Wildlife Service Headquarters

Splays (pg 62)
Roseate Spoonbills Feeding; Photo: Corey Douglas, U.S. Fish and Wildlife Service Southeast Region

Here Be Puffins (pg 70)
Maine Coastal Islands National Wildlife Refuge; Photo: Author

Mangrove (pg 76)
Mangroves in River of Grass; Photo: G. Gardner, Everglades National Park Service

Sage-Grouse (pg 88)
Malheur National Wildlife Refuge; Photo: Author

Milkweed and Monarchs (pg 96)
Monarch Butterfly; Photo: ©Marilyn Barnes

Synchronous Firefly (pg 106)
Fall Color from Luftee Overlook on Newfound Gap Road; Photo: U.S. National Park Service

Glacier (pg 114)
Jackson Glacier, Glacier National Park; Photo: ©Samuel Silver

Painted Desert (pg 122)
Petrified Forest National Wilderness Area North Unit; Photo: National Park Service

Fumarole (pg 130)
A Fumarole in the Devil's Kitchen Hydrothermal Area (Lassen Volcanic National Park); Photo: LassenNPS

Conks (pg 136)
Tree in Reed Canyon; Photo: ©Marilyn Barnes

Muskox (pg 144)
Denali National Park; Photo: ©Marilyn Barnes

ABOUT THE AUTHOR

Theressa Silver is a freelance designer, teacher, and author. She has designed for magazines including "Jane Austen Knits" and "Enchanted Knits," and indy yarn companies. She is a contributor to the Knit Picks Independent Designers Program. She also has an array of self-published patterns available on Ravelry under the name ArgentGal Designs. Theressa is a biologist by training and the influence of math and science can be seen in many of her designs. When she is not knitting she likes to be outside kayaking or hiking. She has been known to stop on the trail, stare at something for a bit, and then exclaim, "I bet I could knit that!" She lives in Milwaukie, OR with her husband, son, two cats, and a dog, all of whom occasionally participate one way or another in the knitting process.

Theressa (aka Mom) at Glacier Park Lodge
Photo: ©Samuel Silver

ABOUT THE PHOTOGRAPHER

Marilyn Barnes began taking photos when her grandchildren were born and quickly developed an interest in nature photography. A self professed "details person," she has a wonderful eye for texture and color and takes spectacular close-ups of plants and animals, many of which she sells as note cards. Over the years some of her favorite subjects, besides her grandchildren, have included roses, birds, butterflies, and dragonflies. A knitter of fifty years, when she isn't behind the lens of a camera, she's likely to have a pair of knitting needles in her hands. Marilyn lives in Milwaukie, OR and can be found riding her bike around town with her camera safely tucked in her saddle bag, or at the local coffee shop knitting with the girls.

Marilyn at Cape Lookout State Park, OR
Photo: ©Dale Barnes

www.ingramcontent.com/pod-product-compliance
Lightning Source LLC
Chambersburg PA
CBHW041220030426
42336CB00024B/3406